ALL OF THE OTHER MARKETING BOOKS ARE CRAP

This is what you need to know to maneuver through the depressing shitshow that is your professional life as a marketer. You're basically screwed. The only thing you can control is how you think. This book can save you.

You're welcome.

Dedicated to Rich, my Gibraltar.

You bought this book because I made you.

You were vulnerable to my title because you're desperate. You're searching because you're trying to learn something, anything, and apply it to the shitshow that is your day-to-day existence. Your day-to-day existence is full of people who aren't as smart as you but still derail you. Passive-aggressive fucks. You have a boss who's screaming at you about goals that are pulled out of his or her ass, with no basis in reality. Sniveling coward. You look around, and there are 1,000 things that are wrong with every process, every paragraph, every column of numbers, every deadline, every fucking everything around you. You're asking yourself is it me, or is it this job or this company, or should I just go fucking cook hamburgers somewhere. You're saying to yourself marketing and advertising aren't fun anymore. This presumes it ever was.

And you've bought books before. And they were **CRAP**. They were filled with overwritten theory and 1990s textbook dung that's been warmed over so many times that you feel stupid, like you were ripped off for buying it. You were. Duping authors.

They were also filled with big case studies from big corporations, like Starbucks, P&G, and GM. Yes, companies that have marketing budgets in the hundreds of millions of dollars. Companies that waste more marketing money in a day on a sneeze than you're allocated in a year to work miracles. And then there's you. And whom you work for. Even in a smallish company people on top don't know your spouse's name, and they expect you to spin nickels into gold through sheer will. Management by mirage.

I've been doing marketing and advertising for 30 years. For the record, the job and the industry have both changed dramatically and have stayed exactly the fuck the same. I've been client-side with a Fortune 100, owned an advertising/PR firm and a strategic marketing firm, and held the title EVP of Brand Strategy with an ad agency of hundreds of people. This book is what I know to be true. Its purpose is to help you.

The chapters are topical. No need to read from the front; read what you want. There's content here for everyone: marketing directors, CEOs, advertising people (including creative types). It's meant to get you through your day with something actionable that makes your world better. So you don't sell out or give up or bang your head against a bottle of Glenlivet so hard that you drown in sticky, delicious tears.

So there. Have a nice day.

WAIT, THERE'S MORE ...

I'm emotional about the topics because I have deep-seated beliefs relating to the business of marketing. Here's one that's at least plausibly delusional: Great marketing people and advertising people are the smartest, most powerful people in the world. Smarter than scientists. Smarter than educators. Way smarter than operations people or coders. *Wait ... you're comparing marketing people to, like, physicists?* You bet I am. It's because we, of all professions, are required to live in precise harmony of left and right brain to prosper. When we don't live in precise harmony, we fail as a result of arrogance of either logic or emotion. I would suggest to you that the smartest person in the world is balanced, poised in perfection, yin-yang'd, with a multiple of power that comes from nothing short of living in the divine Zone of the rational and the creative. Flow. It's the marketing communications Zone. And the Zone is a cultural force, molding people's life experiences through products, services, and belief systems like no other influence or discipline in modern society. We rig elections. We direct culture. We make people healthy or sick, give them psychoses, make them cry on cue, adorn their heroes, and deplete their financial well-being because they spend money on what we tell them to like on Facebook. And we do it en masse. We're merchant Jedi, and we fucking manipulate the DNA of society. Believe no less.

Yep, if you're reading this book, that's you, at your powerful essence when you're your best self. Now, with all that power, do tell: If you're client-side in a marketing department, are you viewed with disdain by other departments? Do they not understand or respect anything that you do, thinking it inconsequential? Nay, even silly? Do they think the company prospers because of product or service or history or credentials or clicks or (God forbid) sales or some other overrated myopic tool that you use? They're all toolers. **TOOLS IN YOUR TOOLBOX.** But you swing the hammer, baby. Your creative side is rare, and if you touch it like tantra you can move the world. Feed it with rational consciousness, and you can make movements happen. Other non-marketing people are jealous of you, because you, at your essence, are mysteriously perfect and powerful in a Zone sort of way, and they know it. They're not just jealous; they fear you. The hairs on the back of their necks stand up when you walk into the room because if you got your act together you could make them question their every truth, and they know it.

I believe this and will give you tools to act on this power during the course of the book. I'll show you how to move closer to the Zone.

Advertising people … back in the day, ad people historically defined culture, not unlike what Leonardo and Michelangelo did for the Renaissance. *Now you're comparing advertising people to the greatest artists of Western civilization?* You bet I am. Leonardo and Michelangelo were paid performers, commissioned by clients, to bring visual metaphor to society to advance point of view. Can you name an artist, like, an actual artist, from 2005? 1995? 1980? Of course not. The best you can do is go to the 1960s, before the boom of commercialism, and even then your artist is LeRoy Neiman or Peter Max, a boxing folk artist and a hippy illustrator popularized by 7-Up advertising. Or if you're really cultured, Andy Warhol, who's famous because he made iconography of soup can graphics, which was homage to commercialism as art. Art of our life, the metaphorical reflection of our beliefs, values, and preferences, has been advanced by advertising people and commercial designers. So advanced is this reflection, that it's no longer a reflection, but, rather, a spoon feeding of predictive behavior to needy audiences waiting to be told what they're culturally supposed to like.

Now, not only are advertising people (mostly strategists, writers, and art directors) collectively the greatest influencers of modern-day culture—get this—ad people can also be credited for single-handedly preserving the U.S. Bill of Rights. Advertising, frankly, is the only thing that separates us from the old Soviet Russia. *Where on earth is this going now … ?* Ad people created differentiation and gave individuality freedom to prosper. Without differentiation, there simply is no choice. Without choice, the individual ceases to exist. The depressing grocery shelves of Cold War Russia were stocked without choice: no ability to choose between Stalin's sardines and Lenin's sardines. Life was generic, low cost, without differentiation, and without advertising. Advertising separates us from monopolization, and monopolization is one step away from stripped-down conformity of culture, politics, ethics, and quality of life.

So next time you buy generic toilet bowl cleaner, think of that.

Do what I say in the book. It's real. And it all fucking works.

DISCOURSE ONE
YES, WHERE YOU WORK IS FUCKED UP

You're not alone in failure. Every marketing entity I've ever known has been fucked up, whether it's a client or an agency (agencies have their own set of business/operations issues that make them as fucked up as clients). I'm a universe of one, but I've witnessed the work of 200 marketing departments. They're all fucked up. For every published case study of successful marketing or advertising, there are hundreds of failed campaigns, muffed trials, and fumbled ideas if there were ideas at all. These aren't published, so you don't know about them.

There are four possible reasons why you and your department feel like you're fucked up and in a state of perpetual failure:

1. Your CEO doesn't understand, support, or participate in the marketing function

2. Your department is inadequately trained

3. The marketing effort is underfunded

4. You have an inappropriate definition of failure

SO YOU'RE A CEO, HUH?

First, kudos for picking up the book. It takes guts to admit you have something to learn. People think it's easy. It ain't. Being a CEO is tremendous pressure, thankless, and lonely. It's especially hard if you're a CEO in a "small" business (under $20 million in revenue), because you've got one foot in the sky, one foot on the ground, and your soul leveraged to a bank that holds your loans. If you're an MBA, I apologize for dissing you, but I'll blame your graduate school for focusing too much on accounting and not enough on strategic thinking and brand development.

The lessons in this book will help you in particular. In fact, much of the strategic disciplines discussed are really **YOURS** to embrace and are championed by the marketing department. Companies need to play offense and defense at the same time. Marketing departments have a predisposition to play offense, with revenue generation via product growth their preferred play to run. **YOU**, however, have to add plays to their playbook: interfacing marketing with R&D. Filling niches with new products and services, enabled by operations. Giving marketing the blessing to throw an occasional Hail Mary. You also have to outline the defensive scheme for them: helping them project the paths of competitors. Concepting zone formations that guard against competitive end runs. And, frankly, giving the occasional speech on blocking and tackling.

If your organization's large enough to have a VP of Marketing, you can expect them to think like a head football coach on your behalf. If you've got a marketing director with scrappy support staff with 1,000 things to do, it's likely that they're thinking more about getting the uniforms washed than the season itself, which means that you, the CEO, is the one who needs to get your head in the game.

CEOS ARE TO BLAME

As a rule, I really don't like CEOs, as I've not met many I respect. Correction: It's the system that I don't respect, and CEOs are byproducts of the corporate system. Most commonly CEOs rise to the top of organizations through the management strata, usually by way of either operations or sales management. Most of them have an MBA that they wear like a neon hat to somehow pass themselves off as marketers. But they're not marketers. They're mostly managers. And managers are not leaders.

Management, by definition, is an observational process that looks at past conditions, usually through numerical benchmarks. If it was quantified in any way, it was measured and reported ... thus, a reflection of past activity. It's likely that your CEO jumped to the top by reducing costs and/or increasing sales in some manner. And what's wrong with that, you say? Well, those people make decent corporate presidents and good COOs, but they make lousy CEOs.

CEOs, at their best, are visionaries. They inspire people to see what doesn't exist. They create internal culture. They honor customers and prospects by bringing them relevancy. They don't ask "Why?" They ask "Why not?" They move an organization forward to a beautiful place, a place conceptualized in their own bountiful imaginations.

The way an organization moves forward is through **VISION.** Usually, a CEO's vision. Does your CEO have vision?

How to tell a bad CEO: If you don't know where the organization is going because they haven't told you or they haven't figured it out themselves, they're a shitty CEO. And by virtue of their silence, they've just made you a shitty marketer. Like a good QB in football, CEOs make position players look better or worse than they really are.

The relationship a CEO has to marketing should be stronger than any other departmental relationship because it's marketing that does the heavy lifting of pulling an organization forward. This doesn't mean a CEO should be a micromanager. They have no business micromanaging anything. They should, however, make it clear where the organization is headed long-term, so that the brand can be evolved over time to reflect the organization's path.

HOW IS APPROPRIATE CEO INVOLVEMENT DEFINED?

Well, one's first instinct is that it somewhat depends upon the size of the organization. Most of what you read in marketing books (the other books on the shelf, the books that are **CRAP**) are based on practices of mega-companies. The case studies are of brands you know, and they're mostly consumer-focused. The reality is that most companies in the world are business-to-business (B2B) and have relatively small marketing budgets. But in both instances, CEO involvement should be the same.

Regardless of size of organization, regardless of whether it's B2B or consumer, healthcare or technology, product or service, profit or non-profit, the CEO should do the following:

1. Define organizational mission and vision (two different things), and communicate those in colorful detail to the senior marketing staff

2. Make sure the marketing department understands the landscape of equities and liabilities of the organization, and understands current and competitive threats. If you, as CEO, don't have a handle on these things, get a fucking clue because you're a blind squirrel

3. Check in. Update. Be realistic. And be available. So many CEOs won't give the marketing department the time of day, except to give them outlandish and unsubstantiated numeric goals out of their asses and expect marketing departments to achieve them, with budget cuts. (If you're a marketing person, you're nodding your head in frenzied agreement right now, perhaps with your fist in the air.)

The truth that CEOs must embrace is that marketing is a CEO's best friend. Not like a dog kind of best friend but a foxhole buddy kind of best friend. So many CEOs look at marketers as the spenders; the people with the crazy ideas; the people who, if given the budget, will just spend it. *(Yes! We'll just spend it! That's what a budget is! The more we spend the more the organization benefits! And, sometimes, unless we spend more to reach critical mass, what we do spend would be wasted! Spend, spend, spend! Spend every damn dollar dammit!)*

When done well, marketing will make a CEO look great, like a 40-year old Richard Gere walking into a boardroom with a $20,000 custom suit and a briefcase full of million dollar ideas. It's all *presentation* and *framing conversations* to boards, customers, non-customers, and employees. That's what marketing people do: We make targets think favorably of the organization before the conversation begins. Then we define the conversation for relevancy in our favor, so closing the sale is easy, whether that sale is internal or external.

If you're a CEO, stop doing shit yourself and buy your marketing department some beers. Then get out of the way.

YOU WORK WITH THE NEEDY BECAUSE NO ONE IS TRAINED

If you're client-side, chances are you have a BA or an MBA in business with a marketing emphasis. You may have taken some advertising classes, where you read about ads, such as Volkswagen's "Lemon" or something from Nike (an organization that curiously doesn't believe in advertising but has produced everyone's favorite ads). Or you worked for your company for a long time and moved through other disciplines in the organization, such as customer service or sales. Any way, you're needy, because there was never a class or a training program that told you how the real marketing world worked. Sorry. The dirty secret is that it's chaos; you live in a tornado of tasks; and occasionally a dung heap hits you in the face out of nowhere at about 100 miles an hour, requiring you to eat shit. Shit eating usually leaves a bad taste in your mouth for a long time.

Most marketing departments are task-oriented because there are few academic venues to learn relevant strategic thinking. So managers embrace tasks, which often translates to tactical solutions to strategic problems. The result is ineffectual marketing and CEOs with lack of confidence in their marketing departments.

It's a sad state of affairs when marketing managers desperately reference Sun Tzu's *The Art of War* as the justification for their ideas.

I've actually seen it a lot, literally. Not that it's a bad book—it holds up well for being a few thousand years old—it's just that fondness for it tends to be reflective of a lack of strategic process training in the individual and no formal strategic process within the organization.

Lots of smart people don't do well at strategy because it's inherently based in the unknown. "Is there basis for that thought?" No, it's the future. People who feel comfortable imagining future states and operating in future state realities are rare. Working forward into the unknown is much different than reading about a strategic case, which is working backwards from a known state into what seems duh obvious.

Beyond strategic training, there's a common client-side void in "execution training." Damn Apple! Damn you to hell for creating the Mac! Internal marketing departments have ballooned into mini-advertising agencies, and the expectation is that they can execute as well as real advertising agencies. They can't. Why? The issues are *quality, knowledge,* and *process.*

There's certainly a time, a place, and a budget for in-house work. Just like there's a time, a place, and a budget for the outfit you wear when you clean a garage. *(Oh, back off haters! Suck it up and read on.)* But if you think you can create communications in-house as good as an outside entity that specializes in communications, you, my friend, just haven't been around the block. You get a pass because you don't know what you don't know, but I'm telling you now that whatever you're doing in-house is adorable. Like middle-school-science-fair adorable compared to what a real agency can do.

Remember, time and place. Just don't bring adorable to a cocktail party. Or to a product launch, where you have the opportunity to lose millions of dollars or get eaten by a competitor because you brought homemade to the market. This makes your coworkers look like failures and could ruin their careers. Know when in-house is appropriate—nay, preferred—and when to call in bigger guns.

QUALITY While the computer has opened our eyes to new highs, it has delivered new lows and has expanded the world of dreck. Dreck, also known as the wasteland of mediocrity, has made us lower the bar on "good," simply because there's so much dreck out there that our ability to distinguish and define good from bad from ugly is impaired. Does your internal team live, breathe, and monitor every ad that makes it in awards annuals and weekly "best ads" sites? Does it seek out the case studies of campaign successes across multiple disciplines? Does it constantly review trends in consumer and B2B behavior, color correction, photographic effects, neuromarketing, and cross-platform digital campaigns?

Fuck no, of course not. Because internal departments have too much to do, and if they have free time, they're better served studying their particular business sector. But any agency worth its salt studies the *communications* sector and will deliver an executional quality advantage over the in-house output because of that currency.

Note in that last paragraph "worth its salt." There are lots of bad agencies out there that don't do anything to stay current. Avoid them.

KNOWLEDGE There are many facts, seminars, videos, blogs, and books (you're reading the best one, as the others are **CRAP**) available for those with a thirst to learn, except that true knowledge is based on experience and intuition. And much of it is in the devilish day-to-day details; agencies learn via osmosis.

Over time, an agency deals with so many situations, such disparate challenges, that "what works" and "what fails," "what's cool and fresh" and "what's dated and hackneyed" become wisdom that's inherent to agency people in a blink of an eye. Internal departments are simply not presented with the same opportunities to develop this kind of high-octane intuition.

Again, not your fault but don't kid yourself in thinking you know what you're doing. It's like the classic war movie, when the new lieutenant hits the black rocks of Iwo Jima and thinks they can take out a pill box by leading a platoon that's been there awhile. You know what you know, and they know what they know. Learn from them.

PROCESS Running an advertising agency is no easy task. I was humbled by it every day and did it for decades with the sector's most gifted players. Agencies also enjoy an ongoing influx of new ideas and new people who bring the best process ideas from their former agencies. Process improvements are constant, specific to the creation of marketing content. But most client departments have very few systems in place to manage workflow from strategy to execution.

Deluge is common. Internal departments are overwhelmed. Last-minute email blasts. Website updates. Golf outing posters. Every salesperson's most important presentation ever. It's not an internal department's fault that they're asked to do more than what they're trained to do or are gifted to do or are inspired to do. Expecting internal departments to overachieve is a strategic error. It's the central reason why marketing departments fail. Successful organizations are honest about their limitations and outsource expertise accordingly.

THERE ARE TWO WAYS TO BUILD A BUDGET OR PRICE AN INVESTMENT INITIATIVE:

OPTION ONE:
This is what I have ($$$). How much does that buy?

-or-

OPTION TWO:
This is what I need to accomplish. How much does that cost?

That's it. If your thought process doesn't follow either option, you likely follow the most common way that most organizations proceed: Ass Backwards Budgeting (ABB). ABB follows "logic" something like this:

This is what we spent last year, so this is what we'll spend this year.

-or-

We expect a 10 percent increase in sales off of the same budget as last year.

-or-

The budget doesn't increase, but we'd like you to expand your marketing area by five states.

--or--

You just need to do more with less. (Back to ground zero.)

STOP EXPECTING MORE FOR LESS. JUST STOP.

There's a point where "more for less" is mathematically unattainable. But marketing departments have been squeezed, squeezed, squeezed as CFOs and CEOs inappropriately view marketing as a classic variable expense rather than a seed for short and long-term revenue growth.

What happens after ABB is that management either forgets about the goal (because organizations lack follow-through, and few people actually finish anything), or marketing departments are tagged with FAILURE. Given that the life expectancy of chief marketing officers is the lowest in recorded history, it's likely the latter.

That's not the CMO's fault.

It's human nature to make improvements on what was done in the past as a means of moving forward. But when budgets are stretched in marketing—as the costs of media and services rise, and the number of options available to communicate with prospects balloons—you can't tweak the same thing you did last year and expect anything with double digits other than loss. You have to tear up your plan and start over with new strategies to spend the money.

LOWER THE FUCKING BAR

Oh, this is bullshit. Lowering the bar as a recommendation? YES. I'm suggesting lowering The Bar. Maybe even burying The Fucking Bar in the ground and covering it with the ashes of marketing directors who lost their jobs because they woke up at the wrong place at the wrong time.

The Bar is the Emperor's New Clothes that no one seems to want to talk about. CEOs think the double-digit increase is a reasonable expectation. Yeah right, 20 percent every year. True growth is about share (meaning, you take it away from some other company like yours that's trying to hold on) minus sector growth, and it's crazy hard to pull off. True growth in the double digits is rare unless you're a start-up.

An extremely common mistake made by American businesses is having marketing efforts led by someone with the old-school title "Sales and Marketing Director." HUH? You might as well call them "Director of Deep and Wide" because you couldn't find two diametrically opposed skill sets presumably under one roof. Consider these definitions:

Sales:
A transaction process between two entities ... like what hookers do.

Marketing:
An awareness and understanding connection based on group messaging ... like what porn does.

Yes, sales is to marketing as what hookers are to porn. You will never forget this. Porn generates awareness, interest, understanding, and motivates people to fuck like rabbits. Hookers have sex and get a commission. Same broad category, but two different roles and skill sets. Don't mix the two if you want sustained satisfaction.

Double-digit increases in whatever numbers you prefer (for sake of conversation, let's say sales) commonly happen for three reasons:

1. Organizations suck at something and get better (the silver lining of suck)

2. Technology gets adopted, and customers get a temporary hard-on

3. Your competitors close their doors, and/or the sector itself has significant growth, which means you get fuckin'lucky

The number of organizations that suck at remedial things is astounding. No diss; it's just that when you're agency-side you see the internal workings of a lot of companies. Hundreds in a career. So many are well meaning, but, shit, a remarkable number of companies are surviving in spite of themselves. They're fucked up. That's the honest truth. The marketing workforce is thin with talent, and operations is often worse. How would you know if your staff is good if you've got limited comparative exposure? If your agency account director is looking at you like you're part of a bunch of monkeys, the possibility exists and would explain your banana cravings.

When improvements are made in organizational blocking and tackling, because an organization sucks at customer service, lead generation, fulfillment, pricing, or any number of marketing basics, guess what happens? Double-digit growth. That's not the kind of marketing we're concerned with in this book, but it should be acknowledged that if you suck at the marketing basics, the strategic content in this book may not help you. Get to work on fixing the holes in the roof before you start tearing pages out of *Dwell* and ordering cement countertops.

Companies have realized exponential increases in profit attributed to marketing because of the relative adoption of new technology platforms, which, frankly, has been screwing up performance metrics attributable to marketing for a couple of decades now. Double-digit gains in productivity and ROI became an expectation because we basically went from candle power to light bulbs. How many asterisks can be put on individual years? Every year there's a new website, a new app, better experience design, or some digital something that lowers bounce and automates transactions. And every year in the future, there will be a new *de rigueur* platform until implants allow us all to think about buying something and it's purchased through brain waves (follow the money to the singularity). Each technical innovation will provide a bump in growth as customers adopt, but organizations will go broke trying to hire competent coders. We're all in a zero-sum free fall in that regard, and true marketing performance will continue to be hard to isolate.

And then there's how most organizations see double-digit growth: They're fuckin'lucky, also known as stupid in context. Example: An agency may say "Our digital department has contributed 11 percent to agency growth this year, whoo hoo!" when the digital development business nationally for agencies may have grown 20 percent or more. A few years ago during one of the many waves of brick-and-mortar chain retail closings, surviving stores would pick up the slack. It wasn't anything but the misfortune of others that made sales rise. If organizations had Directors of Common Sense these things would be pointed out during times of strategic planning and goal-setting as aberrations rather than marketing wherewithal. But I gotta say, it's hard to beat fuckin'lucky. That which you don't control, but are in a position to benefit by, is opportunism by another name.

So bury The Bar. Stop obsessing about growth because it's pompous, realistically unpredictable, and arguably unquantifiable. In the cases of carbon paper companies, family-owned pharmacies, the music industry, and network television, they've redefined success as "survival."

Can you make shit happen? Yes. You can make crazy shit happen. Crazy fucking shit, beyond numbers. Long-term loyalty. Perception change. Buzz that you ride like champion surfers. Nothing feels better than success. You **CAN** make things **NOT FUCKED UP** in your own professional world and create positive improvements in the manner in which you work, the engagements you have with colleagues, and the outcomes of your livelihood. Read on.

DISCOURSE TWO
NOT THAT IT MATTERS, BUT THE AGENCY BUSINESS IS FUCKED UP

If you're a client, your first instinct is to think that you're getting ripped off by your agency. Fair enough. Entirely possible. Most organizations feel the need to defensively take care of their own. It's human. Agencies will do what they can to make money beyond what's obvious because clients want favors for doing business beyond the services they contract for, for as little as they can possibly pay. So, maybe, depending upon how you frame it ethically, somebody's ripping someone off. Or it's just the give-and-take of business.

The primary cause is not that agencies are bad; it's simply because they're in the resource-allocation business. And that business is a no-win. It starts with new business and the process of choosing an agency, which has been absurdly fucked up for a long time. Combine that with the fact that clients now tend to have multiple agencies (rather than one integrated shop), and you have agencies spending a disproportionate amount of money on winning business, reducing their ability to deliver a quality product or service.

Since metaphor is a rapid means to communicate a complexity (hey, sounds like advertising), let's imagine a restaurant business. You, as a hungry patron, contact several restaurants, each with its own perspective on food. You tell them very little about your palette preferences, allergies, or how hungry you are. You challenge them to serve their best meal gratis. In return, you'll consider bestowing the honor of serving you more meals later, those of which you will pay for but will likely haggle on the price. And you still want appetizers and drinks for free.

This is called an agency review.

Or, consider this: You're a master chef, with great food and what you believe is a fantastic dining experience, but your food spoils unless someone eats it. And you're having trouble even giving it away because people say, "I get my food somewhere else, and what if you poison me?"

This is called a sad waste of talent, and the frustration that agencies have in trying to be proactive in soliciting trial.

Agencies aren't making money anymore. And creative people (in the broadest sense) need to eat. We writers, designers, photographers, and generic creative folks don't think for the pleasure of it. We think for food, shelter, and kids in college.

Compound outrageous new business development costs with the fact that the whole message delivery system is changing, and you have a recipe for strain. Agencies are faced with learning new skill sets when the old skill sets aren't entirely ineffective, just passé. Clients are looking for the new, hot segmentation system for Hispanic profiling; the new, hot anthropologic planner; and the new, hot algorithm because they're all … new and hot. Agencies are pushed to keep up, even though most small-to-mid ad budgets don't scale appropriately to new and hot. Big $20-plus million clients can get a lot of free meals from big agencies willing to take a risk. The "free" costs will be buried somewhere later. But if you've got a smaller budget and are working with a smaller agency, the agency cannot serve you for free or offer tastes of new, hot services without starving itself.

FIGURE OUT WHAT KIND OF AGENCY YOU NEED

Do you need a full-service agency that integrates PR? Do you only need design? What level of strategy do you need? Are you willing to pay for quality?

Agency services are not commodities. There's good/better/best for all functions in the agency world. And, frankly, their relative costs are likely driven by how much the agency pays people to do the work and how they factor overhead. Proactive people cost more. Experienced people cost more. Brilliant people cost even more than experienced people. NFL tickets and fishing trips cost more. If you go from Agency A to Agency B because you want to improve the quality of work or the "freebies" in the experience, then expect to pay more.

Culture is also important. If your internal culture is collaborative, pick a collaborative agency. If you're a dictatorship, pick a similarly structured agency. Believe in any ideals? Like "do the right thing" or "balance work and family"? Or "just do it?" Why you like an agency at the onset is likely because you responded to it culturally rather than rationally. Conversely, why you eventually end up hating them is because you're culturally on different planets, as well, also known as hating every little thing it does because it irritates the shit out of you (divorced people will understand this).

> The whole reason we're talking about agencies and clients in a book about strategic doctrine is because of the Zone. Ultimately, the Zone can be defined as clients thinking more like agencies, agencies thinking more like clients, and everyone thinking more strategically.

ENGAGING WITH AN AGENCY

Historically, no one cares what agency relationships were like in the '80s or '90s. They care about engaging now. But history has an odd way of recycling, and, like fashion, elements of the agency relationship that worked in the past will be found to work again. A prediction, but you heard it here first.

"Partnership" used to be the key component to most agency relationships in that agencies were true extensions of client-side marketing departments. As marketing departments grew and clients thought they could do everything cheaper and better themselves, the dependency on agencies to be "go-to" for a variety of services was reduced. Interaction declined. The flow of information to agencies was altered to "need-to-know" status. And, naturally, an agency's ability to "add value at every turn" died. Clients blamed agencies for being order-takers and not being proactive. Agencies that once viewed their client relationships as marriages now felt like part-time housekeepers in the homes they built. So much for carving the turkey at Thanksgiving. Agencies are at the kids' table, if considered family at all.

> The real problem that agencies have with clients is passion. If you start an agency, or work at an agency, you do it because you give a shit about your craft. You give a shit about making the next great TV spot or the next great magazine ad. You constantly marvel at the work of others in your field, seek out their work, learn from them, and motivate yourself to grow. Agency life is too hard; the only way you choose to do it is if you give a shit. Hey, clients, can you say the same? Do you give a shit about what you do? Or, are you using "busy" as an excuse? The dirty secret is that agency people resent you for not caring.

As the commoditization of new technology happens, and it will, the concept of "partnership" and "marriage" will rise again. Having experienced both "best-in-class" interactions and integrated partnerships, marriage was a positive, win-win way to do business. First you engage, then you marry, then you grow businesses together. But it starts with trust.

Trust starts with sharing information. Fear of information theft has left clients giving agencies only partial information, and agencies, in turn, are delivering partial results. Agencies then don't know if you distrust them, if you don't have your act together, or if you're stupid. If it's either of the last two, tell them, "Hey, we're so fucking stressed out and busy we have no clue on what to do next." It takes five minutes. Then your agency can help you.

If you're a client, here's how you share information:

1. If you have a budget number for a project or campaign in mind, let the agency know. Money is epicenter of nearly every agency conflict. This isn't poker, this is business. Don't play "read my mind." It's demeaning. Work together

2. Make your agency smart with what you know. If you've done research, give it to them. Most agencies sign non-disclosure agreements in this spirit. Agencies also need to know what you know in case you don't know much. They'll round out your knowledge. Secondary research is everywhere, and agencies will do due diligence to find it. If you don't want to pay for them to find out what you already know, share it, otherwise agencies will get secretly mad at you because they may feel the need to do uncompensated research

3. Share your objectives. No, not just, "We'd like this campaign to generate X in sales" (which, by the way, is a goal not an objective because it has a number) but "We're positioning ourselves as a unique provider of X service in this sector." If you don't know how to develop a strategic objective, keep reading this book to the end

HOW AGENCIES MAKE MONEY

Well, we've already established that agencies are hard up for cash. But agencies do make some money, don't they?

First, a very simple primer on the theory of making money at an agency.

PEOPLE TIME Hourly rates generate the greatest percentage of revenue for agencies. Agencies charge more for senior people than juniors, but make more money on juniors relative to salary and benefits. They can also get greater utilization from juniors, meaning agencies will work them until they quit because juniors job jump to gain experience and make more money anyway. That's why some clients perceive "bait and switch" because no one shows up for new business meetings with 22-year-old kids out of school. (Not that there's anything wrong with 22-year-olds; they have a legit perspective.) But the higher the quality of the agency the more likely its reliance on senior staff to actually work on your account (and the higher the cost). These days, senior staff is now anyone with five years experience or more. Ten years gets you a department head position because most people don't hang around that long. It's too hard.

Utilization and capturing all time that people spend working on a given account or project, tied to an estimate, is key. It's not factory work, but the agencies that are making a significant profit from hourly rates run it that way. Many agencies require their rank and file to bill 90 percent or more of their time to clients, which, frankly, doesn't allow for much of the fabled ad agency drunken fun time. (FYI: 60 percent utilization means everyone's comfortably busy.) Seniors get a bit more of a break with utilization, but freedom comes with a price: When agencies get into trouble, department heads are often the first to go. Not many people get to retire from agencies.

Culturally, in agencies that rely on "people time," if they're doing financially well it's likely that if four hours are allotted for a layout, someone will come by at 3:59 and say "it's done" regardless of whether it's "done" or not. Agencies like this can be horrible places for creative people to work, but such is the price of fiscal health. As a client, you get what you pay for.

MARK-UPS Procurement departments of larger clients have created havoc with mark-ups. It's a rare business in any sector that doesn't mark-up goods or services bought on behalf of clients, but it's common for larger clients to negotiate "no markups on purchases" in their contracts. Bastards! It's not that agencies make that much money on mark-ups, but it was a place where agencies felt they had a little cush on a job when unexpected things happened because unexpected things are, ironically, predictable. The old standard agency mark-up is 17.65 percent (mathematically equivalent to the 15 percent commission). The bigger the agency, the bigger the client, the less likely mark-ups are a component of compensation. For smaller agencies, they're important.

I was never fond of agencies marking up their own internal time, but some do. Their justification is that if they could outsource services (such as web coding or retouching), it's justified to mark up similar services if kept in-house. Whether an agency marks up internal time is an appropriate question to ask in the review process.

Then there's the hidden mark-ups ... yes, you heard it right. Money is still buried in the form of kickbacks and finders' fees. Money is also buried in complexity and innovation. Was it right for programmatic media purveyors to overcharge clients (likely because they were burying software development costs)? Programmatic overcharging was one of the biggest scandals in the agency business ever. Money is also buried in favors and will always be. Clients want favors, agencies want favors from their vendors, and their vendors want favors from … sorry production houses, you're the end of the line and have no one to hit up, so you're screwed.

MEDIA COMMISSIONS Agencies still buy media, but it has gotten messy. New "media" channels based on the web have altered compensation structures, along with brokers who promise lower rates on traditional media from bulk buying. Larger clients usually go with firms that do media only. Small to mid-sized budgets are still best served by an agency that also provides media plus creative and production services. Agencies will charge a commission based on purchasing, retainer, or hourly rates for services. Commissions are commonly four to 15 percent, but it's rare. Most clients think buying media is gravy for agencies. Actually, new channels and analytics have made media buying more time-intensive than ever. They're not the cash cows clients think they are, and it's not unusual for agencies to lose money on media buying because of the old-school paperwork. So much is still done by paper.

And please, if you think that agencies do creative and production for the compensation obtained from the media commission, you need to advance to the current decade. You're two or three behind.

I wish I had said this, but the credit has to go to one of the greatest clients of all time (his identity is being protected here but think "athletic shoes"). He said, "The best day of your relationship with a client is the first day. It goes downhill from there." Indeed.

REVENUE SHARE, SALES INCENTIVES, AND OTHER URBAN MYTHS Everyone always talks about how agencies should put "skin in the game" of their clients' success. Great! Awesome! I've seen clients reach never-before-seen heights in revenue because of the work that we've done—$millions in incremental profit—only to have our budgets cut because they "didn't need to market anymore." A share of the bounty instead of financial punishment would have been fantastic! The problem is that most clients want agencies to reduce fees in exchange for bonuses, which would be akin to reducing an employee's pay so that they would work extra hard to possibly be paid more later (with no accounting for the performance of the actual product, economy, or other sales influences). Agencies should have performance incentives based on fair valuations of agency results. But recognize that if you're in a business that has a long sales cycle, or an integrated communications metric, or ego-centric management that think prospects came because of the organization or product itself (ha!), an agency will not necessarily be given the recognition it deserves in a timely fashion.

And last, but certainly not least … **FLOAT** Yep. The money you give agencies is a free, no-interest loan if you're paying them for media and expenses. That's it, that's what many agencies exist for. Agencies of about 100-plus people who buy media make bank in interest annually because they take your money and manage it, commonly paying vendors and media properties 90 days after they receive invoices, which can be 30 or more days after they bill you. Media buying services are cash management experts as well, which is how they're able to give you reduced commissions. Smaller agencies (meaning smaller than 75-100 people) may not have the kind of volume to make significant direct-to-bottom-line cash but likely use your money as a no-interest loan regardless.

This float thing all sounds great but recognize that it just takes one client to stiff an agency on a big media bill, and all the float in the world won't stop the ship from sinking.

THINK LIKE AN AGENCY

An agency's greatest value lies in its brain. Its brain is a repository of every great idea, every visual oddity, every advertising and promotional success in the last 20 years. Agencies know them because they're recycled constantly! Contrary to popular belief, it's truly all been done before.

Which is why I personally laugh out loud when I read blogs or news stories about clients that are lauded as brilliant marketers because they had the idea of giving away 100 cars or setting up fake vending machines with crazy interactions for anyone who puts in a dollar. Brilliant? No. New? Hardly. Agencies have so many ideas like that they trip over them in the hallways. Clients are not brilliant because they initiate ideas. Clients have guts because they initiate ideas. The vast majority of clients want to do everything without risk or effort, so agency ideas drown in cowardice. Cowardice is the plague that keeps our collective world mediocre.

Agencies are naturally wired to think big, while clients are wired to think small. Home runs versus bunts. Clients live in a Six Sigma, tweeky, definition-of-quality-via-lack-of-variation world. Agencies look for big ideas because agencies know big ideas produce big results, and all clients say they're looking for big results (like people say they want an exotic life of sex and adventure and sports cars, but really are content to read about those things on websites).

Thinking like an agency also requires you to think like a prospect and not a client. This does NOT mean thinking like a stupid person. Most clients think consumers and customers are stupid. Yes! Clients, beaten down by lowest-common-denominator problems and complaints in everyday operations assume that the entire prospect pool they communicate to is just that: irritable and stupid, requiring remedial communications. Not true! Agencies are experts at getting into the mind of the customer (that's exactly what planners do) and, if creative teams are worth their salt, actually base creative on what targets say and think and do, regardless of whether the prospect is six years old or 76. Most heavy consumers of products and services are NOT stupid. Disengaged, disinterested, and non-committal, but not stupid. Limited world view but not stupid. So where clients think people are dumb, agencies know people are just bored.

Thinking like an agency is also a bit like thinking like a physician. If you go to the doctor and say, "Give me a bandage because my cut doesn't heal," it's akin to going into an agency and saying, "I need a half-off direct mail piece because my sales are slow." Your cut's not healing because you're an undiagnosed diabetic with low white count, which means you could have cancer, and your sales are slow because your brand is dead animal clogging up your revenue colon. Agency malpractice should be instituted when they give you your direct-mail piece without doing other diagnostics, and, frankly, your company deserves to die a slow, painful death if you didn't work with your agency to identify your real problem and take action on it.

Agencies live a life of problem-solving. They're good at that. Now, if you're saying, "My agency just throws superficial tactics that cost money at my problems, and that doesn't work" then, well, tru dat my brotha, my sista. It's possible that your agency doesn't have the information, or the acumen, to solve deep-seated business problems. The information would be yours to share, and the acumen formula is, frankly, this book plus experience. Not every agency's mission is to be in the Zone, or well-rounded in its approach to problem solving (design, interactive, and PR agencies are specialists, for instance). But full-service agencies should, in theory, be able to add problem-solving value in honest ways that internal resources cannot. And, as a side note, if you believe that a design, interactive, or PR solution is all you need to solve complex business problems, in addition to the dead brand animal you have in your colon, you would also be full of shit.

DONT'S OF THE AGENCY REVIEW PROCESS

Somewhere somehow someone once wrote that you can get a lot of free ideas if you have an agency review, and ask participating agencies to do speculative creative or a speculative plan or a speculative budget.

I'm tracking this person down with hounds from hell as you read this. This person needs to be taken out for the good of society.

There are 100 things evil about this approach, among them that the approach has driven up the price every agency must charge its current clients, which, in turn, has driven up the cost of every product or service in America, which, in turn trickles down to what you individually can or cannot afford in every given day in your personal life. All wasted, without benefit to anyone anywhere. Even the client who receives the speculative work in the end gets little benefit at all, factoring confusion, misdirection, and misinformation. It's intoxicating, yes, to have people give you ideas for free, but it's also disturbing if you remember that we're all working to feed our families.

The "winner" of a speculative situation is usually the agency that spends the most resources, rather than the agency that's best suited for the client and the assignment. It's human nature, and clients are human. One agency will usually have the best creative, another the best overall "presentation," another the most buttoned-up analytics. How to choose? Most clients choose based on "they wanted it more," or "that finished look," even though it's extremely rare for speculative creative to actually be produced for use. The additional downside to spec work, especially if you're a local client in a local review, is that you create a whole lot of bad feelings in your own backyard.

> **Real story …**
>
> **Reporter interviewing an agency head (me):** Do you do spec work?
>
> **Agency head (me):** "Yes, we spec to be paid for it."

(FYI: I stole that line from a good friend. Plagiarism is the essence of culture.)

When I had an agency of 25 people, we commonly spent more than $70,000 in resources pitching a juicy piece of new business. Larger agencies commonly spend much more. Multiply this by multiple pitches, and it can be an agency's downfall regardless of whether it wins the pitches or not. To label this a "cost of doing business" is disproportionately unfair. This "cost of doing business" requires compensation, and an agency puts itself at risk unless it factors commensurately higher rates to make up the difference.

HOW TO PICK AN AGENCY Pick an agency by first meeting with the partners in their own space. Listen to how they speak about their culture, their mission, their favorite marketing, their most-valued relationships. Give them a list of your needs as a client. Give them an idea of the budget you'll spend with them and the level of service you believe you'll need. Look at their work and their case studies. Ask them about relevant experience. Ask them if they can share, in detail, one integrated campaign they managed for a client. If you like them, like their answers, and get a good vibe, ask for another meeting. Meeting two should be at a bar. It won't include the agency partners but rather the account team that likely will be assigned to your account. They should have no decks, no videos to show you. Meet the account team, meet the creative team. Then, **PICK AN AGENCY.** Do not pick an agency based on how it presents. Do not pick an agency based on how it writes documents. Pick an agency based on how it'll achieve success working with you. Then pay it fairly. And when the agency does a good job say, "Thank you," and mean it.

Is this pro-agency? No. It's pro-common sense. And it will save your ass if you're a client. Because you'll pick the right agency.

When you're calling an agency with regrets after your review, be honest. Agencies who are honest with themselves have concluded that 90 percent of clients are cowards because they always play the "it was a hard decision and you came in second" card. Be truthful and give the agency some constructive criticism to help them in their next pitch. If your answer is "We were confused, everyone used the same words, and we made our decision because we didn't like the beaten down AE or the rude robot from your digital department," SAY SO. Have some balls. Agencies can take it. And need it.

DISCOURSE THREE
HOW TO THINK. WHERE TO START.
HOW NOT TO FUCK YOURSELF.

There are a variety of people who may be reading this for which I'm grateful. There are likely people in the ad business who represent many disciplines: creative, account service, PR, digital development, strategy, user experience, media. There may be clients: CMOs, brand managers, marketing directors, coordinators, CEOs (ah, sorry for all of those bad things I said about you—if you're reading this, it probably didn't apply to you). Professors and students might also take a read. It's my intent to bring something to all of you that you find valuable for the rest of your lives.

HOW TO THINK

I've held many job titles, but mostly in the last 30 years I've led brand development at the onset or close to the identification of a marketing opportunity. Much of this was true brand development rather than campaign development, but the principles that drive the approach are essentially the same. Thinking is seeing, and seeing the future is strategy. There are two parts to being good at strategy: 1. Getting high enough, like 30,000 feet on a clear day with no turbulence, to see pathways. 2. Believing in creating what doesn't exist, which is at the horizon. This second part, belief in a future state that doesn't exist, is what makes some smart people suck at strategy. It makes them suck at change. And it makes them suck at leadership. These people see their shoes and focus on past steps and next steps. Progress is slow.

Leadership and management aren't the same. Management is inherently a backwards process: *"Here's what to do, based on what I believe you can do, based on your past performance. Okay, did you do it? Now spend time to give me a report on what you did."* It's likely that your thinking has been framed by tangible past performance rather than the ability to deliver future possibility. This behavior modification makes you more likely a manager rather than a leader. Which, in turn, makes you unable to run.

No diss. Not everyone can lead/run, so you may have a DNA or BDD pass (that would be Beaten Down Dog; as an animal rights activist I hate the metaphor, but you get it). Good leaders usually make shitty managers and vice versa. Business needs both, and both deserve respect for their roles in the marketing process. But when professional people who are good at their craft (creators) are promoted to managers, and leaders are given management (rather than leadership) responsibilities, the shitshow is in full force. It's why you hate your job and your day-to-day world seems broken.

But wait, wasn't there talk of the Zone? The perfect balance between left and right brains, management and leadership, vision and profit, offense and defense? Yes, my friend. It's about learning how to think. If you learn to think this way, always, you'll live in the Zone, and it's a very fulfilling and prosperous place whether you're a leader, manager, creator, or master schmoozer. When the ability to think strategically is implemented and adopted in organizations, it has the power to shut down the monkey carnival that's making your work life miserable because it diminishes focus on repetitive tactical execution and wasting time on shit that'll never see the light of day. Eventually this evolves into what's is known as "common sense."

Accomplishment is a positive force. It's intoxicacting. Your ability to think is what you can control. Focus on it and be prepared for drunken nirvana.

THINKING IS ABOUT SEQUENCE

Have you ever had someone tell a story by starting in the middle? You wonder, "Am I stupid?" You try to track, and they keep going on and on in chaos, and you're forced to do either one of two things: Stop them and ask them to back up as you recap your understanding, or walk away mumbling, "What the fuck was that? I have no idea what's going on." They're peeling the onion from the middle.

Sequencing and bucketing content in context is a discipline you should learn and defer to immediately when problem-solving. If you practice the iterative steps in this discourse enough, it will become part of your automatic memory, and you'll dazzle the people around you with your ability to rationally justify every idea you have and every move you make, whether the ideas were of your own invention or part of a group process. This is because your ideas will come from strategy and not what unwritten rule or post/podcast influenced you in the last 24 hours. You will actually have marketing ideas, be able to captivatingly communicate those ideas to others, and won't be cowering in fear of being thought of as a poser.

THE 360 OF TRUTH IN THE BUSINESS OF LIFE

First, understand that truth is relative. It's why we have crazy divisions of belief in our world. Your truth is not your colleague's truth. Everyone's truth is based on relevancy. If someone's a product developer, her truth will be "quality product is why we have customers." If someone heads a call center, his truth will be "we interface with customers, and the fact that we care is our differentiator as a company." Both valid, both likely wrong.

A college president once told me that being a president (presidents are managers, CEOs are leaders) is like being a mayor: lots of constituencies and perspectives, combined with the responsibility to acknowledge all points of view and enable the greater good, even though "good" isn't necessarily positive for every citizen. Strategy, as suggested by the training of 80s gurus Al Reis and Jack Trout, is (paraphrase) a discipline of compromise and exclusion. But individual truths are real and shouldn't be excluded. If people's perspectives are diminished in the compromise and exclusion process, they turn off and good fucking luck getting them to stop talking behind your back from now to the day you quit. You work in a small town! In a small world! In addition to being a way to develop strategies on your own, the step-by-step process of thinking outlined here is also a blueprint for team thought and corporate harmony. Team thought will be the focus of this discourse because while you easily could be neurotic yourself, it's primarily other people who are fucking up your work happiness.

HOW TO THINK: STRATEGY FOR TEAMS

1. CONFIRM YOUR TEAM IN CONCENTRIC CIRCLES

Garbage in, garbage out. Remember that? It's true when it comes to collaboration. Yes, we have to be inclusive of all truths, but at the risk of metaphor abuse here's another truth for you: Small teams get shit done and large teams don't do shit. So when a CEO says, "Include Tom, Dick, Harry, and all the Heathers," that's politics not strategy. Democracy is inefficient, and business can't be a democracy or you'll be out of business. That's why concentric structure is important to manage both volume of content and player engagement, both when strategic planning and implementing.

Snuck that strategic planning thing in there, didn't I?... Yes, *strategic planning.* Don't skip this discourse because you hate strategic planning or think it's not what this book is about. Strategic planning in its most formal form is a solid basis for the infrastructure of thought that can be applied to any problem-solving exercise. So learn this process first and then scale it for campaign planning, operations planning, and any old meeting you need to have when you have to figure out a solution with multiple people whom you dislike. This process can be used for planning a wedding, political campaign, new product launch, or a junket to Mars. Seriously. It's how to think in its most diamond-like brilliant form.

AT THE START Both invite participation and limit participation.

Yes, you need to involve people in your little project—everyone you likely don't want to. If a small group of cronies walks out of the room having built the greatest, most sparkly, and powerful Holy Grail ever and declare it to their uninvited colleagues, it will fail. Fail, fail,

fail. Because unless people believe they personally have equity in the input, decision-making, or creative process, they'll dismiss every great thing you and your friends come up with. And potentially tag you as self-serving snobs. If you're client-side, that means your sales people won't sell how you want them to, your manufacturing heads will disregard the spirit of your specifications and function as robots just to spite you, and your boss will personally blame your small team for egregious cross-discipline communications failure.

If you're agency-side, it means your internal creative chiefs, account chiefs, or client marketing chiefs will politely listen to what you have to say and then **CHANGE IT ALL.** Acknowledge and ignore. They'll spitball ideas of their own until your idea is dead, covered in their body fluids. Because they weren't part of it, and they think they can have better ideas in a minute than your team can have with weeks' worth of work. Maybe it's true, maybe they can. But you need to overcome their immediate dismissal, slow your presentation down, and present these people with a basis for your creativity that includes indisputable strategic basis.

Do you remember kids on the playground who were just little shits? Nasty, rumor-mongering, let-me-trip-you-as-you-walk snots? They grew up, and they work down the hall. There have been multiple long-term studies on the nature of group dynamics in the contemporary workplace. The revelation? "Be nice." Yes. Nice people collaborate well, and assholes are assholes in a group, on their own, when they were kids, and will be assholes until the day they die and go to hell with all of their other asshole friends.

Your first concentric circle to input is the widest net.

For purposes of example, let's use this challenge:

A REBRANDING CAMPAIGN FOR AN ESTABLISHED BUSINESS-TO-BUSINESS PRODUCT/SERVICE This happens all of the time because like every modern person, products need to stay current (so, yes, get your hair colored and buy some new kicks—you're a product, too). Whether you're a client-side department or an agency working on behalf of a client, you need input. You're not supposed to make shit up. You're not in the fiction business, and you have to make sure what you eventually suggest is believable, rooted in organizational pillars, has business relevancy, and can co-exist with operational realities.

So if you're a client in this little party, and this is a significant rebranding, you need to do a SWOTT.

Whaaat??? The tired old SWOT? Wait a minute, this book has a typo! There's two Ts! *Where's the fucking quality control?* The SWOTT is the sneakiest way alive to get participation from dozens of people in an organization without actually acknowledging them face-to-face. It's a brilliant, without fail secret weapon of extraordinary long-term defensive power ... ammo in YOUR hands.

Why? If you're doing a rebranding campaign for the company you work for, there are people in your organization who think they have a voice in what's said about their beloved company. If they can type, they think they're copywriters; if they had crayons as a child, they think they're art directors; and if they ever had an idea about price, product, promotion, or place, they think they'd be a better marketing director than you. Everyone thinks they can do your job. (They can't, they just think so.) In addition, they think they're the ones who know your organization's corporate realities best because whatever line they're on is, to them, the front line. You need to get their opinions, however impotent, or they'll never buy what you're selling internally. On the positive side, some of them might just have an insight or two that you may need to change the game. So, listen.

The hardest thing about the SWOTT is not the collection but the analysis.

Some gross generalizations:

1. People like to bitch, and it's easier to go negative than positive. Expect Weaknesses to be twice as long as Strengths

2. It's common for Strengths to be Weaknesses and vice versa. For instance, "Lots of young people with new ideas in our organization" might be both positive and negative, in that it requires elder wisdom to know how to factor new ideas and channel those young'uns. No elder wisdom? Preponderance of elder dogmatism? That's called culture clash

3. People run out of gas when filling these things out, plus they have a problem with OTT because it requires them to think and not just observe. In general about

15 percent of people are strategic, meaning they can put two and two together, and envision a reality that's not clearly sorted/marked or doesn't yet exist. Leaders do well at OTTs, followers not so much

As a client, the SWOTT is sort of your job. The content is something you should have and keep current because frankly *it's your damn business, and it matters!* As an agency, you can easily offer to manage this for the client and create a layer of third-party anonymity. This also makes you a tiny bit more indispensable because you know the client so well and sometimes find some good OTTs that you can turn into proactive insights.

Whom, exactly are the participants we're talking about here? District managers. Sales leads. VPs of Every Disparate Thing. Even soldiers in the trenches. Write a lovely email about how the process is happening, and while everyone can't participate at every step of the process, their anonymous input would help. Say that at appropriate points in the process you'll keep them informed of how everything's unfolding. Say they're hand-picked because of their value to the organization. And stay true to your promises.

If you don't know how to structure a SWOTT (usually administered by online survey), use this simple guide:

STRENGTHS
List your organization's (or product's) strengths. Strengths are primarily internal or reflective of the organization's position within its marketplace. Bullet points not paragraphs. *Examples: Great quality. Long contract terms. Outstanding training program. Low turnover. Market share lead in an SBU. High awareness among CEOs.*

WEAKNESSESS
What are the weaknesses in your organization (or product)? Weaknesses are primarily internal. These are things that may impact successful performance in your marketplace. *Examples: Crappy quality. Lack of differentiation in competitive set. Poor return policy. Inconsistent customer service. Old-school technology. Underfunded marketing.*

OPPORTUNITIES
What opportunities, either internal or external, currently exist? Opportunities include improving a weakness, capitalizing on

a market trend, or a identifying competitive weakness. *Examples: Cross-sell training. Geographic expansion. Investing in ecommerce. Competitor closing. Adding internal FTEs.*

THREATS

What are threats to the business, either internal or external? Yes, this could include "Bob in accounting because he's a sloppy dick." *Examples: Underperformance of the sales department. Increases in operations costs. Product liability. Limited talent pool. Competitor expansion. Market saturation. Environmental changes.*

TRENDS (HA! The second T!)

Trends can be internal or external. Trends are anything that can be tracked over time, quantitatively or qualitatively. *Examples: Margins getting squeezed. Increasing revenue via ecommerce. Younger workforce. Social media becoming more of a force. White papers as means of establishing credibility. People quitting in droves. Climate change.*

Why the fuck no one incorporates TRENDS, the second T, in this world exercise is beyond me. This is probably the most important checkpoint because it's predicting future and is prime fodder for strategy. Actually, you probably never heard about the second T, which is why. So from now on, two Ts it is, and say you saw it here first.

As I write this, I'm sitting in an airport, and I see a woman with a packet of papers that has MODULE: VISION and BRAND WHEEL. Cute. I used to be like that ... all branded and enthusiastic about my modules. People who go through my facilitated days, in the end, come out inspired and smarter than when they walked in. But nearly everyone in processes such as these enters as a cynic. Ditto with the nouveau "game play and improv your way to marketing greatness." That's just got too much artificial sugar. Nobody's life dream is to be a marketer. We do this because we have to make a fucking living, and beachcomber doesn't get you a company BMW. The cynics are right, so make your process efficient, on task, and, most importantly, EXECUTE the plan you come up with or it's all a waste of time. That's why most people are cynics. Planning is easy. Doing is hard. Cheerleaders don't play football for a reason.

Findings from the SWOTT are summarized, disguised (take away catch phrases so it's truly anonymous), and presented to your smallest concentric circle as part of the active, collaborative planning.

You've now activated everyone in your largest circle. And shut them up.

The SWOTT is information gathering, but savvy researchers are quick to point out its failure: It's all opinion. There's nothing wrong with opinion as long as you look for consistencies of thought; depending upon your universe, limit official reporting of what's said to "it makes the presentation if three or more people said it." The SWOTT is bulleted and presented for leadership review during the first workshop collaboration day either as a grid-like document or old-school, printed and revealed with much fanfare on big Post-it® brand papers stuck on a large wall. Frankly, there's something charming and engaging about doing it on paper. Most people think it's a hoot.

Here's another prediction about what you'll learn from your SWOTT: Employees, regardless of title, know next to nothing about competitor marketing, operations, or pricing. Which makes positioning and competitive analysis (coming soon) really hard to do with just internal opinion. And makes you, because you understand the context of where your organization lives in the marketplace, unique and valuable (first step inside the Zone, my friend).

SMARTCRAP.COM   **SWOTT**

STRENGTH	WEAKNESS	OPPORTUNITY	THREAT	TREND

You can download this diddy, built in a Microsoft® Word file, at SmartCrap.com.
FREE! Because you already bought the book.

2. GET YOUR INTEL IN ORDER

The SWOTT is a reality check of opinion, which is perception. Opinion and perception are obviously important; some people consider them more important than reality. What someone is manipulated to believe is true is true (let's not talk politics here … that's potentially another book). But for now, step two is about gathering actual facts.

HISTORICAL AND CURRENT NUMBERS Strategy is about business performance, but if you don't integrate Key Performance Indicators (KPIs) into your planning, it's like showing up for baseball practice without a glove. Why organizations do this—and they do it a lot—is beyond me. "Oooooh we hold it all close to the vest," they say. Then hire Stevie Wonder as your Uber driver because you're lucky if you go around the block without running into a pole.

Figure out what you can share and **FUCKING SHARE IT.** We're talking revenue, profit, units, whatthefuckever gives your CEO a jones. Keep in mind that remedial types will just say "sales." Sure, okay, but there needs to be greater specificity to that: Sales from who/where/ what? New customers? Former customers? Cross-sell? Sales units? Gross revenue with no regard to costs of goods sold? Break it down, clients. If you don't know, admit it. And agencies, have you ever thought to ask for this kind of numbers detail before a campaign? Shame on you for being superficial order-takers if you haven't.

CHEAP-ASS PRIMARY RESEARCH Research companies do a nice job—love you all!—but if you're a normal marketer like 80 percent of the businesses in the U.S., you're scraping together nickels to make fire. Why would you spend 50 grand on research when 50 grand is like half of your budget for brand development? Unfortunately, this is why a lot of research companies are going out of business: the DIY mindset and the lowering of the bar on academic discipline. Sigh. Sorry. But let's be clear what research really is: getting people's input. For a lot of organizations, CheapAss may help identify places for more formal information gathering or it may be enough.

After three decades of doing consumer and B2B research, here are some truths about people:

- People want to give you their opinions, but they don't know what to say

- People think what they have to say is relevant. It usually isn't

- Most people are brand-aware but brand-don't-care. Meaning, brand ambassadors are rare. They exist, but it's hard to base an actual marketing plan on them. Clients who put too much stock in brand ambassadors to do their bidding tend to be cheap fucks

- Take research as it relates to R&D with a grain of salt. People don't know what they want and have no idea about what they could have in the future. Go back in the past and famously no one ever said "I want an iPod"

- Most people can't even remember the names of brands they care about with $200 million advertising budgets

So why ask anybody anything? Good question. Don't. Unless you want to know if they're unaware or aware, don't ask people questions. Observational and anthropological research, now that's another thing ...

Designate a planner, AE, or Generic Agency Smart Person (could be anyone) to get on the phone and talk to the top five salespeople who sell the product or company, and the bottom five salespeople. Even if products are consumer-facing, there's a juncture in the sales chain that's business-to-business or direct. Ask them about their challenges, what works, and what they would do to make the product or company better. Ask them about perceptions. Promise anonymity. Write it all down.

If it's business-to-consumer/retail, go to the place where the product sells. Hang out. Watch people buy the product. Notice how they do it. Do they just throw it in a cart without thinking? Do they read the label? Do they stand there dumbfounded with two products in their hand? Do they go online in the store to get info or find a lower price? Do they ask anyone in the store for help? Are the people who help appropriately versed in your product? This is remedial shit but really important.

If it's a pure ecommerce play or in any way sells online, it's pretty common for the digital types who manage conversions to overcomplicate their knowledge base to protect their jobs when speaking with mere mortals (definition of "mere mortal": anyone who's not in charge of Google Analytics, code, or fixing your computer). No diss on digital, but we're talking marketing and the relevancy of digital behavior to strategy and messaging, which is still product/service/economic engine-based. At this point, eschew the granular. Can you sit with an online chat person? Can you talk to an online chat person about what customers say? Can you talk to the people who process returns? Can you look at sales data based on the user's experience in making a transaction? What metrics are charted, and how do they trend? Are there metrics for engagement or just sales? Can you organize the relevant points on a prospect's decision journey and conclude anything? (Or, do you have a shitty website and can't even do any of the above? If so, just put this book down **NOW** and go get a better website.)

Can you call the last five organizations that purchased (or didn't purchase) the product or service—like, for instance, say it was a healthcare organization that bought online bill pay software—and ask them some questions? How long had they been thinking about the decision? How many providers did they review? Did they find them by internet search? Did they review their products on websites? How many Requests for Proposals did they manage? What process did they use to evaluate providers? How did they finally make the final decision?

Do you have a SurveyMonkey account? Do you know you can build surveys and import email lists? Do you know SurveyMonkey has a database of people who will take your consumer product survey? Do you know that Google provides lots of online intel, including competitor data, for free (go to thinkwithgoogle.com/tools, and spend some time)? By the way, I'm not a shill for SurveyMonkey —there are other very fine services that are fantastic values. SurveyMonkey is just DIY cheap.

SECONDARY RESEARCH Regardless of your sector, there's this thing called the internet, and it's got a lot of info for free or nominal cost. In fact, it has so much information available that it's nearly impossible to make sense of relevancy and quality, even if you're a professional researcher. If you're a client and don't know where to go in your sector for specific intel, start with trade associations. Also research competitors, Google the agencies that handle the other companies in your sector as there may be case studies on the agency sites. If you're not checking Google Analytics on the daily, start immediately. If you're an agency or a client on steroids, you best be checking sites such as WARC.com (it has a searchable database; membership, but you can buy specific content if you find an abstract you like) for case studies, insights, best practices, and just about every deck presented at every seminar ever—which is insanely cool. It's broad and worldwide but inspiring. Other tricks: find a college student from a big school's business program, pay them an intern's wage, and ask them nicely if they'll use their school passwords to access premium secondary research services such as Mintel, Iconoculture, and TrendWatching. Is this illegal? I don't know. I apologize if it is and have never ever done this myself. Or, even better, buddy up to the bar and pay for subscriptions to these services. Most offer generous free trials to see scope (including WARC).

3. TAKE THE DAY OFF

Not really. But you're going to invite a small team of important folks to get off-site for a day or at least hang in a room at work for a day to process. As soon as you say "off-site", everyone gets squirrelly. What's with people thinking that off-site working is a boondoggle? It's NOT. It's more efficient, productive, and collaborative than people trying to multitask at work. Off-site makes people feel special and empowered. And it gives this process the tag of "important." Don't forget the snacks.

Why does team collaboration fail? Ego and insecurity. People whose first priority is to keep their jobs play defense. They hunker down, as if the planning process is designed to expose their weaknesses (to be fair, it does, but it's not the primary intent of planning). Why is it a shitshow? Because everyone's sitting on toilets, cultivating their own production, and enjoying their own scent. Instead, you all should be running. Fast.

If you're scaling the sequences outlined in here for a campaign or a smaller project, then obviously you don't need a full day, multiple days, or even three hours in a row. If you're rebranding your company, you need more than just a day, and anyone who gives you shit about that is a blustering fool. This is grueling, mind-fucking work. The word "day" means six hours of work, some lunch, some breaks for addicts to access their phones, and maybe a cocktail at the end. Don't laugh; after a long day, if you schedule beers or margaritas, and chips to show up at 4 p.m. you'll get another hour out of people, and the content will be enlightened.

If you're doing a true retreat to get high-level work done, size matters. With more people, you have to change structure and have more facilitators. Large retreats (15 or more people) are a whole different thing. They're less about strategic thinking than they are about input and inclusion. A strong facilitator can use the opportunity in a larger group to teach and lay foundations for eventual strategic conclusions, but that's a fucking other book (dang, there are a lot of books that need writing ...).

Here are some ground rules for your meeting. Publish them.

Leave rank at the door.
No mobile phone usage. Breaks only.
If you're not going to contribute, don't come.
No bad input.
Keep it short. No grandstanding.

Now you're thinking, "That's all fantasy. Bahahahahahah! Our CEO is a rude fuck. He looks at his iPad when he's not taking over every meeting; and intimidates everyone until they sit silently, nodding approval of anything he says." Yes. True. Which is your first real strategic decision: to invite, or not invite, the CEO or other high-powered contrarian rude fucks.

Back in the early days of strategic planning, before I learned a few lessons, I would always demand that the CEO be present for every minute of planning that had to do with corporate rebranding or SBU branding. I've learned now that that depends upon the CEO. Unless you're some fucking huge company, they should absolutely be involved, up-front and at the end of your session. But you may want to keep them out of the middle if you're doing a full day. If you're using modules to figure out a campaign or marketing course of action, they absolutely have no business attending. It's not their job. It is, however, your job to communicate what you're doing up front so he or she knows that collaborative recommendations are on the way. Your CEO should be smart enough to figure out that he or she would be a dirtbag not to engage positively with whatever the group created.

Here's how to invite participants to the group meeting. Keep it under 10 people if you can. Don't invite them if:

- **You don't respect their knowledge base.** If they bring nothing to the table, then you don't eat

- **They monopolize the conversation.** If you must invite them, the moderator has a "bullshit bell" and rings it when they need to shut up. Not a metaphor. Get a bell

- **They're just quiet.** People need to speak. If you have three people who speak in your group and three people who don't, then you have three people in your group not six. There's no value in people "seeing the process"

- **They're just fish out of water.** For the love of God, admit it. Some people are just not cut out for this. Don't invite people because they're nice. Saying people are "nice" means they've got nothing else going for them

- **They're cynics who just bitch all the time.** Naysayers think saying no or reminding people how things don't work makes them smart. On the contrary, it makes them look lazy or like cowards on a power trip. Next time you confront one of these negative fucks, quietly think about that in your head. It'll be like fresh lemonade for your soul

FIRST: WHAT'S THE VISION?

If you take away one thing from this book, or do one thing out of all of the tried, true, and great recommendations here, this is it. Don't be cynical that this is old-school. Don't be thinking it's just line items from an existing three-year plan. It's not. It's everything that's important in the form of numbers and states of being, internal and external. Visioning is slowing down the subconscious thoughts of your true desires until the molecules of energy become matter. It's an astral projection of your life, your company's life, in all its beautiful possibility. It's a way to see the future. It's **THE VISION**, and the vision is you and your team's moment to articulate to the universe what it is that can be achieved with luck, logic, execution, and money. Don't worry if you currently have no luck, never heard of Aristotle, can't block or tackle, and are flat fucking broke. It doesn't matter. *The future has yet to be created.*

Get a big sheet of paper. Big. NOT A WHITEBOARD. A big, 6-feet long by 4-feet high sheet of paper. Cut it from a roll available at an art supply store. Or piece it together with six 22-by-28-inch Post-It® sheets (tape the backs together). While you're at it, buy some artists tape, which looks like duct tape (or Duck™, which is a brand) but usually doesn't take paint off the wall. (I've destroyed rooms. My bad. You should probably test your tape a week in advance because if it peels off nicely on day one it'll take paint with it on day five, so don't leave it up in a war room unless you're okay with being yelled at for destroying property.) Get some Mr. Sketch® Scented Beveled or Broad Tip (that means not pointed) markers. *Do not get any other markers. These are the best markers in the world.* They're everywhere, like Walgreens. Tape the big paper to a flat wall in your retreat room.

Why not a whiteboard? Because people are trained to put drivel on them. Whiteboards are for farts. What's written down in this process should be meaningful. Paper means you can keep the Vision, move it to a war room or a CEO's office, and hold your organization accountable to it. The new whiteboards that print are nice, but they print to an 11-by-17 inch piece of paper. Useless for this.

Write **VISION** and a date that's three years in the future on the top of the big paper. Three years because it's far enough in the future that you know anything can happen but soon enough that you know you have to get your act together. Work for a hospital? Three years. Work for a tech company? Three years. Work for a company where the sales cycle is 18 months? Three years. After trial and error over the course of decades doing this, three years is the optimum time for humans to give themselves a pass on tomorrow's responsibilities and allow themselves not to get into the existential morass of a Woody Allen dilemma: *"The universe is expanding, so what's the point?"* Also, while climate change is also real, Western civilization likely won't be totally fried in three years, so there's that.

If you're the leader of the process, let's hope you can print fast and big, and draw simple cartoons. The first group exercise you're going to do is to fill your paper. You can practice by learning these before you start. Impress your friends!

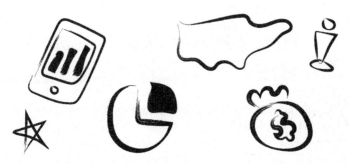

So the Vision goes something like this: You stand in front of your group and say, "Fill up this paper! What does our world look like in (fill in the year) if everything in our world is fantastically successful, like fucking (okay, don't say "fuck" unless you have a culture where it's okay to say "fuck") uni-fucking-corns of success and joy? What defines that?" Then you take 45 minutes to fill up the paper with everything they spit out, from assorted KPIs ("We go from 10,000 units to 18,000 units!" and draw big numbers with a big arrow up) to cultural imperatives ("We have Pizza Thursdays!" and draw a pizza) to competitive maneuvers ("Our largest competitor, ABC Company, is out of business!" and draw their logo with a circle/slash through it) to curiosities ("Our CEO keynotes our industry's big trade show and people think we're really smart, and we all get new, better jobs!"). Put it all up there. Use four-ish colors of your deliciously scented markers.

These become your goals and objectives, and the definitions of success for your initiatives. Flags on Everest. The rest of the process is to figure out which of these are important, at some level attainable, and how to get there from here.

Now take a 15 minute break. You deserve it.

SECOND: PRESENTING THE INTEL, SWOTT, + RESEARCH

Feeling all on top of the world from the Vision? That'll pass.

Remember that SWOTT you conducted, and got the opinions of Tom, Dick, and Harriett? It's time to share. We talked about collecting your SWOTT content previously and how it's important for inclusion, which allows you to sell in your program because you've made people feel involved. Well, perception is reality, and SWOTTs are about reality, as defined by the opinions of your largest concentric circle. Is the collective consciousness correct? Maybe 75 percent right. But what a 75 percent it is! While this should be an organization's responsibility to do, you may want to consider contracting with a third party, such as your agency, to collect and scrub this info. Because it's like 50 people lit shit and put it on your doorstep, and that's kinda hard to deal with if you're a relatively small company. Now, that said, it's important shit, and it can power a lot of successful evolution.

The content you're presenting here is abbreviated, sorted, and grouped. I like writing it on the easel-size Post-it® sheets and revealing it section by section. People are extraordinarily attentive, so you'll need to go slowly.

Remind the group that in order for a bulleted point to have made it to the Post-it®, three or more people must have said it. This shuts people up. Makes them thoughtful with the gravitas. Embellish the bullet points as you go and remind people that organizations tend to be very hard on themselves. As with any of the SWOTT categories, ask them if there's anything they'd like to add on the fly.

As you move through each category, you'll note that Strengths are also often Weaknesses, and Opportunities, Threats, and Trends are often skimpy. Some bright people will repurpose Weaknesses and turn them into Opportunities. We talked about this before; watch for it.

SWOTTs are great because they level-set reality, especially when it comes to CEO expectations of marketing success. It's usually a slap of cold water that makes everyone realize that foundations have to be laid operationally for marketing success, and that marketing, product, and operations are codependent.

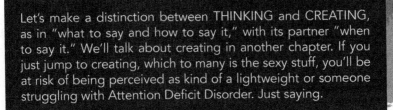

Let's make a distinction between THINKING and CREATING, as in "what to say and how to say it," with its partner "when to say it." We'll talk about creating in another chapter. If you just jump to creating, which to many is the sexy stuff, you'll be at risk of being perceived as kind of a lightweight or someone struggling with Attention Deficit Disorder. Just saying.

Take another 15 minute break. Listen to the chatter! People will actually seem engaged, and will thank you, personally, for doing this. They'll think you're a master spy for not revealing any of this early; little did they know you just finished it hours before and haven't eaten. Keep your swagger and eat a snack in slow motion.

THIRD: TARGETS, NOT CREATED EQUALLY

If you're a marketing director who when asked, "Who is the target for this product?" says "Everyone!," please close this book NOW. Shut it down. Really? You think that? You may be hopeless. There are no products on earth, other than air and water, that should be targeted to everyone.

No marketer has enough money. Never, ever has there been a campaign with enough money. Prioritization of targets is the first step to conserving budget and honing messaging. Targets are not created equally; there's a bang-buck ratio, and you need to figure that out before you even think about actual ideas or execution.

Targeting's function is two-fold: media and empathy. While the evolving future of communications is predicted to not include ads (or so say smartasses who blog), the place in which you deliver your message is called a channel. Broadcast television is a channel; digital display is a channel; social has many channels; magazines are a channel; email's a channel; chalk on a sidewalk is part of in-life, which is also a channel; and so on. If your communications includes expressions in a channel, called **PAID** advertising because it costs money, you need to express your target in terms of how media people are able to sort their buying decisions.

For our business-to-business target, for instance, media is often purchased by Title. VPs of Whatever, Directors of Minions, Chief

Chaos Officers. Titles obviously vary company to company, so as you group your target titles think of them in terms of the content that might interest these folks. Also keep in mind that a company may have multiple contact points who are involved in decision-making within the same organization. Yes, you might want to speak to all of them, but they may not read the same publications or have the same motivations, so your messages within the same campaign may vary (that's the empathy part; read on).

The same principle applies to consumer-facing targets, where media context is even more important. There are infinite options from which to choose for message delivery. How people connect with information is how media is purchased, and a good media planner will look at prospects anthropologically: what is their day like, when are they attentive to what channel, what mood are they in when they connect with a channel? For consumer targets, targeting is still old-school in that it's qualified by demographic data (25-54, M/F/Adults, income, geography, that sort of thing). But life stage, socioeconomic cluster profile, interests, purchasing behavior, and technographics (their adoption of digital life), and moment on their path to purchase or remarketing journey can also be layered into the process of prioritizing targets for budget allocation.

Three Types of Media:

PAID Means it costs money and is actively purchased. Some social channels have pay-to-play components

EARNED Means it's Public Relations, and you got a story placed, sort of free

OWNED Means it's your website or content you placed on social channels that you manage (or pay someone to manage)

Resource allocation, meaning dollars and time, is the game here. What targets have the greatest impact on the buying decision? For B2B, if you ask the salespeople, they usually get all paralyzed and say, "It depends on the organization! Well, that's actually true. In prioritizing your targets, you have to get a handle on your prospects' own internal process for choosing their suppliers/ vendors, which varies from organization to organization.

Did you just get lost on all of that clustering, technographic, path-to-purchase talk? No worries. That's why you need to work with agency people. Agency people reading this knew what I was talking about. If you're client-side and you don't know about all of the ways you can micro-target, it's because **IT'S NOT YOUR JOB TO KNOW.** You're supposed to know about your product and have some idea about what you don't know. If your boss thinks you're supposed to know everything that agencies know, you're vastly underpaid. You're a marketing director who's supposed to know about your product and sector. You're not a targeting tactician for fuck's sake. **This is why you pay people to help you.**

This is a gross generalization, but this book, as complicated as it may seem, is about simplifying thought in a world with too many variables.

Okay, to recap because I've been rambling awhile, our charge is to do a B2B product/service rebranding campaign. Let's just say it's a big product, like the kind that people do an RFP (Request for Proposal) for, as in a software platform (so, like, not staplers). So we're rebranding a software platform for a company that sells these things. And let's assume, for sake of argument, there are a lot of choices for this kind of platform, and it's in the sector of healthcare. Specifically, a hospital system would buy this product to help manage its purchasing.

Dollars for donuts, this is how the process works: A small team of people at the place looking for the software is charged with picking a vendor. The team comes in with:

1. Whom they know based on whom they've worked with in the past

2. Whom they saw in a trade publication or digital display targeted to them

3. Whom their bosses know

4. Whom they've been solicited by

5. Whom came up on Google

Most guests at this little party will likely come from Google because team members will be scrambling to contribute someplace just so they don't show up to the first meeting with their respective dicks in their hands. Then they'll invite all of these companies to submit in round one.

From round one, they'll pick:

1. The safe choice

2. The expensive choice

3. The cheap choice

4. The overtly tech/innovative choice

5. The easy/convenient choice

6. Maybe the cool choice, based on how the companies are positioned in the competitive set

7. The choice of obligation (somebody's brother-in-law). Remember this list for later because it's the foundation for the positioning question: Who are you on the list?

The rebranding campaign that we're working on will be driving and supporting this fundamental law of positioning: One of Each. It's the path by which our software product will eventually be invited to the game.

As we list targets, we need to know who in an organization is most influential at two points in the sales journey: the point where the initial invitees are asked to submit and the point when a choice is made after RFP responses are reviewed. This is important. Those two most influential people should be prioritized high on our list of targets. The rest, forget about them.

And just to do due diligence, ask the team if there are any other targets of consequence. Reporters? Investors? Valuators? Recruiters? Potential employees? Current employees? The brand we create will need resonance here, too. Despite what loud voices say, brand development is not just for short-term sales. Even if you lose at the point of RFP inclusion or in the final tally, your exposure to the prospect team could mean a call after they take another job. Everyone on that team is an important future contact, *and it's your brand that they will retain.*

Now look at the list. Let's say there are six assorted target titles that would be impacted by this rebranding. Assign each a numeric value, one to 100 (100 being of screaming-hot-important value, zero being zero value) so the total of your assignments equals 100, as in what you'd do if you were creating a pie chart. You'll need to come to consensus on which target titles are important to you. This gives you an idea of messaging priority and resource allocation by way of channel management as you move forward. Choose no more than three targets for the next exercise. Two would be better.

Create a persona for your target(s). Title? Lifestage? Ph.D.? Ego? M/F? What are these people like? What motivates them professionally? Legacy? Looking good to their boss? Doing the right thing by way of their company? Doing the right thing by way of their discipline? Notoriety? Containment? Work-life balance? What makes these people tick? Don't know? Find out.

Take a break. Because if you do the next step now, you might not make it out alive.

Often, if you're client-side and in charge of marketing, you're also by default in charge of your team's professional growth. Participating in a process such as this is a big teachable moment, and having your team-members participate would also save time in the long run every time they ask you, "How did it go?" Fair enough. It's also nice to have some mental and physical help. Give them tasks in the process: Note-taking, room dynamics (responsible for refreshments, seating, paper), instant research (if you're referencing stats, for instance, they're responsible for having them at their fingertips).

DISCOURSE FOUR
INTO PUNISHMENT AS A PATH TO BREAKTHROUGH?
THEN THIS IS FOR YOU.

You know that thing that you do that you just hate to do but feel really good after you do it? Run a couple of miles, see your aging parents, do a green seaweed cleanse, that sort of thing? Needs and Motivations is that.

I don't always do the entire Needs and Motivations exercise, but when I do it's the part of the day that makes everything come together. People with divergent truths walk in others' shoes, light bulbs above heads illuminate darkness, and the whole Tao of marketing and operations comes together like 1,000 hummingbirds flapping their whispering wings to create a sonnet of wind. I don't always do it because people hate this part and hate the person facilitating it. Objects have been thrown at me with violent intent. But when people get the hang of it, it's golden fucking sunshine.

So let's go back to the target exercise: Let's say the software rebranding we've been alluding to is a platform for a hospital system's procurement department that unifies pricing. What the dealio it does is when the ER in one hospital orders tongue depressors and their outpatient clinic down the road orders tongue depressors, the hospital system gets the same price and the two purchases ladder to the same bulk contract. *"Yikes," you're thinking, "couldn't you have thought of something sexier?"* Well, this is a real-world example of how this process was used, and most of us don't do sexy work (despite marketing being porn). Rebranding means, in your instance, new identity/logo, new presentation/sales materials, and a trade advertising campaign consisting of digital display ads and a bit of print in trade publications (mostly to make sure you can get some PR from the pubs).

Okay, quiz time. From this list, who's the likely target for your rebranding campaign?

1. CEO of the hospital system because this person will ultimately approve the purchase and has responsibility for overall system profitability

2. CFO of the system because this person is powerful because they're the money thug

3. CIO because what you're selling is really software and an IT thing

4. Head of procurement because it's actually more of a purchasing thing

If you ask your salespeople (remember, you're in marketing for the software company, running this process, which means you're the purveyor of porn and not the pimp who's always selling and works on commission), they'll tell you, "It depends! It depends on the hospital! All of the targets matter!"

So pick TWO, and base your decision primarily on a combination of these things:

1. Who's the **FIRST** contact? Who initiates the RFP or can get you in consideration for the RFP?

2. Who's the **FINAL** decision-maker? Not all decisions are rational. If the process is based on points, don't forget you get secret points everywhere for your ability to manipulate the irrational (that's called "a brand")

3. Who's easy to find via media channel? Certainly your website is accessible by everyone. But for outreach, which target is able to be reached easily via trade advertising or digital?

Based on the criteria, here's how the test stacked:

CEO ‖ WINNER! because he or she is the ultimate decision-maker, and may have initiated the review process, even though someone else took it over. CEOs are easy to find in paid media, too. They like to see their name in print, so go where they can, on occasion, find their famousness or famousness of the people in their circle of friends.

CFO ‖ NO although if you were pitching to smaller companies than a hospital system, CFOs often do double duty as COOs, and they may be more day-to-day in decision-making.

CIO ‖ NO because its likely they have far more important geeky fish to fry, like the whole medical records craziness. CIOs will be involved in implementation, but if they initiated or choose any provider here they'd be severely stepping in someone else's sandbox.

HEAD OF PROCUREMENT ‖ WINNER! because if they're not using something like this, their personal head is at risk to roll. This is their sandbox, and there's negative consequences if they fail at their job, and what you provide will help them succeed. They're also easily found in that their specialty is purchasing, which isn't as broad as the whole big money thing.

BUYERS IN THE E.R. AND SPECIFIC DEPARTMENTS ‖ NO, NO, NO, NO. Don't laugh, though. "The sale" is a very powerful force, and people whose job it is to purchase enjoy the perks of solicitation—it's the equivalent of having someone tell you, "Oh my, aren't you good looking, interesting, and essential!"

So our two targets are the CEO and head of procurement.

Let's first talk about the CEO. Who is he or she? (For ease, let's break the rules of grammar and call this individual "they," and assume we're targeting more than one of them.) Put together a mini-persona to start things off: They're 50-plus, could be a physician or someone with medical training, likely came into the business originally to help people in the most benevolent sense. Hospital CEOs deal with a lot of highly educated smart people with egos (MD stands for Marketing Director, you know). They've learned to out-ego their constituencies for survival.

What about HubSpot, Salesforce, and CRM lead management software miracles?

They're great. Seriously. If you're a B2B company and have "salespeople" who are responsible for trolling and finding potential clients with quantity as a measure, hook yourself up to one of these automation platforms. You should have been doing this about a decade ago. There are a lot of B2B agencies that, for a small fee of like $10K a month, would delight in raking in easy money—I mean, uh, managing your CRM lead management—by way of one of these magical platforms. This is sales management. Marketing's function is brand management.

Brand management means these leads generated by HubSpot get all the right feelies when they're introduced to you (i.e., "My, you're a good-looking brand, and I would love to walk down the street with you, and have people in my organization and competitors say, 'Damn fine, damn fine, indeed'"). Marketing is a trip to the salon, nice dress, new shoes, and the right accessories.

If they're the CEO, they've out maneuvered everyone and made some enemies. It's kind of like politics. They have a lonely, important job, but they drink the finest single malt Scotch. (Have you ever noticed that Scotch is usually capitalized? That's because it's that good. Nobody capitalizes bourbon.)

Put **CEO of HOSPITAL SYSTEM** on the top of your big easel paper. Leave about eight inches of room (we'll fill that later). Write the word **NEEDS** on the left. About half way down the paper, on the left, write **MOTIVATIONS.** Now, remind the group about why you're all together. In this simple case, *"We're here to figure out how to sell our software system that will consolidate various hospital purchasing orders, often initiated by department, into one overall contract."*

Now, introduce the two definitions of **NEEDS** and **MOTIVATIONS.** For this module, we're going to define both as such:

NEEDS Product and service features that are minimum requirements (leave out superlatives, such as "good" or "excellent"). Note differences between simple product differentiation and broader reasons that are connected to the manner in which a prospect does business; also consider that the prospect may not even know that they could benefit from whatever it is you're offering, may not even be looking for whatever it is you're selling, and may not even know that such a thing exists. **BIG HINT: NEEDS** are important during initial information gathering (website) and the RFP invitation stage.

MOTIVATIONS Reasons why the target would choose you/ your offering over some other competitor's offering. Often, these are subjective and become more important as you come closer to the point of transaction. The world is full of parity products and services, and why someone chooses your parity product over someone else's parity product often has nothing to do with you but, rather, what you mean to them. This process is a high-stakes mix of job interview, casting call, and football team roster-filling. In this motivations part of the exercise, you're learning to read minds. **OBVIOUS HINT**: If you can anticipate motivations and learn to adapt, you win.

Under the word **NEEDS**, ask the group, "What does the CEO need?" In the case of this particular assignment—the software system that will consolidate the hospital system's disparate purchase orders into one contract. The CEO's **NEEDS** may look like this:

NEEDS

- ROI that translates to long-term cost savings

- ROI that's easily projected and demonstrated for budget management

- Scalability to accommodate secret merger/acquisition

- Clear articulation of what you're selling (because they may not be aware)

- Clear reinforcement that this software is standard operating procedure of the hospital of the future

Hey look, the CEO doesn't have many needs, do they? They may initiate the initiative, or approve the initiation of the initiative if it bubbles up from senior staff, but they're not the person Googling software solutions. However, they're likely a huge influence on which provider ultimately gets the contract, which takes us to motivations:

MOTIVATIONS

- Demonstration to his/her Board of Directors that the CEO is opps-/tech-current

- Demonstration to senior staff that there's an expectation of collaboration

- Demonstration to senior staff that performance standards are high

- Easy-to-understand language, so the CEO doesn't feel out of control

- Trust in a partner so his/her decision isn't questioned by the Board/staff

- A price that demonstrates frugalness, ability to negotiate, or fairness

- A positive contribution to their legacy

Now, it's tricky to facilitate this kind of process, but part of what you're learning in this book is How To Think. Or, more transparently, How To Think So You Can Shut Down Rampant Stupid From Happening Around You And Enter The Magnificent Marketing Zone.

What you need to keep top of mind whether you're doing B2B, B2C, hospital-to-consumer, non-profit, or **ANY** kind of marketing is that the **FIRST AND ONLY** question that your prospect has in his or her head is—wait for it—*"What's in it for me?"* That's right. Deep in everyone's head, what we all share, regardless of race, creed, sex or stature, is narcissism. Whether you're buying a sub sandwich, choosing a real estate agent, making a donation to a non-profit, or fulfilling a government contract for widgets, the process of provider choice is built on "What's in it for me?" and/or its introverted cousin, "How do I personally feel about that?" That doesn't mean you, the collective You, take bribes or make wrong decisions because you're self-dealing; it means that subconsciously your decision to respond to an outside communications prompt of any kind is first influenced by its ramifications to you, personally. Even in the case of this software platform, if it's "What's in it for me is that I'll be looked upon by people around me as someone who does a good job," it's still a variable with great and enduring power.

Even if you're the most selfless of beings—a mother—your choice of organic baby food is tied to knowing that you've done all you could to deliver the best mushed apples to your baby. And when your children are older and demanding the deliciousness of nutritionally evil macaroni and cheese, as a mother you acquiesce because it makes your children happy and, therefore, you're a great mother (and you can lick the spoon).

So that list of motivations? "What's in it for me?" is the catalyst for choosing a provider.

Now let's talk about the **HEAD OF PROCUREMENT.** Remember, we picked CEO because they would likely have a role in the final decision, and even may have initiated the decision to look for a software solution at the headwaters. And we picked head of procurement because this person (male/female/trans = they) is directly responsible for contract management, and the fact that they don't have a solution in place means that they're at risk for getting fired. The head of procurement's Needs and Motivations paper might look something like this:

NEEDS

- Compatibility with specific legacy software systems

- Replacement of outdated software protocols

- Period of redundancy with current systems

- Scalability to accommodate budget restrictions

- Scalability to accommodate increased transaction volume

- On-site coders

- Guarantees to meet milestones

- Information security

- Data scrub to ensure consistent part/order numbers

- Metrics dashboard

- Future option for inventory management

MOTIVATIONS

- Good customer service at the RFP stage

- Easy to understand RFP

- Increased his/her knowledge; made them look smart

- Trust that the provider makes his/her life easy

- Trust that the provider will deliver on time

- Trust that bosses/staff will believe it's a good supplier find

Both the needs and motivations of the CEO and the head of procurement are decidedly different, right? Hold that thought.

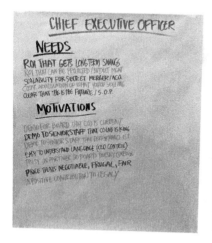

These are what the big pieces of paper look like when you do it for real.

Okay, now look at your sheets of paper (ha! you thought you were done ... oh, nooooo). Some of the lines in the list are fairly long; let's hope you left room on the right side of each paper because you're going to add two columns. The first column is **HOW IMPORTANT.** What we've done here is list messages that might be included in our multi-channel media program. However, all messages are not created equal; some are more important than others, and every member of your consensus team is going to have to contribute to figure out **HOW** important each message is from 0/Zero (meaning just ignore this stupid thought) to 100 (meaning this message is a BFDeal). The whole process of methodically talking about each message is strategy/team-building gold: It gets people thinking, talking, negotiating, and bringing POV. It also creates fights, and then like children who are well-adjusted and not shitheads, it creates an opportunity for individuals to learn how to meet in the middle.

DIGRESS If you talk to copywriters, they'll suggest that you do a brief for a single message and do a single ad for each message because they can't possibly concept to more than one message. This is total bullshit if you're truly talking about an ad. A little digital expression, sure. An ad, like a print ad, can hold three or four. Any more, like five, in a single execution just becomes a stupid jumble. The How Important part of this exercise is an attempt to prioritize which messages are most important for your creative people (and salespeople) to communicate to your prospect.

Back to consensus building: **HOW IMPORTANT** means how important it is to the prospect. For instance, if the team doesn't think compatibility with legacy software is **HUGE**, like, 99, you should get another team. Something like on-site coders, well, nice enough, but it's probably not going to be a deal breaker for any organization, so that would get like a 20.

Now if you've been there done that before, you might be saying, "My team has no business knowing what prospects care about." You could call that the realization that you probably don't invest in enough intelligence, or you have a team that does what it's told and no more. Horses with blinders. Through the years, the lack of intel about prospect needs/motivations, prospect perceptions, and competitive attributes/ liabilities has been positively astonishing. Others have said that formal research, specific to needs and motivations, should be completed prior to any strategic conclusions made by the team. If you have it, this is the point in the process that's shared with the team. If you don't, this is the point where you recognize your lack of intel and get smart somehow. Remember that "choose your participants well" warning? This is where you see the implications of lightweights. It becomes immediately evident if their knowledge about the sector is weak, and this weakness is important as you move forward and decide whom you want in your foxhole.

So let's just say you move on, do the process, negotiate **HOW IMPORTANT** these variables are for **PROCUREMENT,** because you finished it last, and it looks like this:

NEEDS	HOW IMPORTANT
Scalability to accommodate increased transaction volume	100
On-site coders	
	85
Guarantees to meet milestones	
Information security	100
Data scrub to ensure consistent part/order numbers	100
Metrics dashboard	5
Future option for inventory management	20
Compatibility with specific legacy software systems	80
Replacement of outdated software protocols	100
Period of redundancy with currentsystems	30
	5
Scalability to accommodate budget restrictions	25

MOTIVATIONS	HOW IMPORTANT
Good customer service at the RFP stage	85
Easy to understand RFP response	85
Increased his/her knowledge; made them look smart	100
Trust that the provider makes his/her life easy	75
Trust that the provider will deliver on time	50
Trust that bosses/staff will believe it's a good supplier find	90

Think you're done? Nope. Now go back through the list again (at this point it's like a dentist saying, "Hey, let's do a root canal on this other tooth because I'm having a two-for-one sale!"). The second column is **HOW WE MEET IT.** It's how your organization actually meets the need or motivation from a product/service POV. Often people ask if it includes perception; yes, it can, if the perception of an organization doesn't align with its equities, but it does **NOT** include perception if the organization is stealth and has none. Make sense?

HOW WE MEET IT

This is the assessment of your own capabilities. Why does it matter how you are as an organization? Shouldn't you just tell prospects everything/anything and focus on the sale? You would only do this if you're a scared, lying liar. Plus, if you haven't figured this out already, this process is about creating a synergy between what you say, who you are, and how to make people care. It's organizational self-awareness, and honesty is the centerpiece of marketing authenticity.

So now your group is going to go through the list, line by line, and come to consensus about how, in reality, your little software platform does each of the line items on the potential messaging list. Everyone needs to be honest, which means, **DO NOT DO THIS PART OF THE EXERCISE WITH LIQUOR**. Because that'll make people too honest, and people will hit each other. Really. It can be brutal. No one has decorum anymore. We're still working from the **PROCUREMENT** list:

NEEDS	HOW IMPORTANT	HOW WE MEET IT
Compatibility with specific legacy software systems	100	77
Replacement of outdated software protocols	85	90
Period of redundancy with current systems	100	100
Scalability to accommodate budget restrictions	100	95
Scalability to accommodate increased transaction volume	5	90
On-site coders	20	0
Guarantees to meet milestones	80	20
Information security	100	75

NEEDS	HOW IMPORTANT	HOW WE MEET IT
Data scrub to ensure consistent part/order numbers	30	97
Metrics dashboard	5	95
Future option for inventory management	25	95

MOTIVATIONS	HOW IMPORTANT	HOW WE MEET IT
Good customer service at the RFP stage	85	85
Easy to understand RFP response	85	65
Increased his/her knowledge; made them look smart	100	65
Trust that the provider makes his/her life easy	75	95
Trust that the provider will deliver on time	50	50
Trust that bosses/staff will believe it's a good supplier find	90	50

This is what it looks like with the added columns.

HEAD OF PROCUREMENT

NEEDS	HOW IMPORTANT	HOW WE MEET IT
COMPATABILITY W/LEGACY SOFTWARE	100	77
REPLACEMENT OF OUTDATED PROTOCOLS	85	90
PERIOD OF REDUNDANCY W/CURRENT SYS	100	100
SCALABILITY TO ACCOMMODATE BUDGET	100	95
SCALABILITY TO ACCOMMODATE ↑ TRANSACTIONS	5	90
ON-SITE CODERS	20	∅
GUARANTEE TO MEET MILESTONES	80	20
INFORMATION SECURITY	100	75
DATA SCRUB TO INSURE PART NUMBERS	30	97
METRICS DASHBOARD	5	95
FUTURE INVENTORY MANAGEMENT	25	95
MOTIVATIONS		
GOOD CUSTOMER SERVICE AT RFP STAGE	85	85
EASY TO UNDERSTAND RFP RESPONSE	85	65
INCREASE THEIR KNOWLEDGE/LOOK SMART	100	65
TRUST THAT WE'LL MAKE LIFE EASIER	75	95
TRUST THAT WE'LL DELIVER ON TIME	50	50
TRUST THAT BOSS/STAFF THINKS IT'S GOOD	90	50

Okay, now what does this say? Here are some gross generalizations:

- If it's **IMPORTANT TO THEM** (high number) and **YOU MEET THE NEED WELL** (high number), **MARKET THE SHIT OUT OF IT**

- If it's **IMPORTANT TO THEM** (high number) and **YOU SUCK** (mid-range or low number), you need to improve your equities or play defense against a weakness in your strategic approach (talk more about what's good)

- If it's **NOT IMPORTANT TO THEM** (mid to low number) and **YOU MEET THE NEED WELL** (high number), you either have to find a way to show them that it's important or diminish how you talk about it up front. The place for this kind of messaging is farther along on the pros pect's decision journey not up front as a central messaging point

- If it's **NOT IMPORTANT TO THEM** (mid to low number) and **YOU SUCK** (mid-range or low number), then you're cool. Don't talk about something you suck at

Now let's just study the numbers here, from top down, and attempt to say something about the potential relationship here and our software business in general.

COMPATIBILITY This is an obvious need, but if our organization isn't compatible with every legacy system it's sort of obvious that we might want to make that clear somewhere on our website.

REPLACEMENT The reason it's not 100 here in importance is because needs are nearly always being met, meaning every hospital has an existing system that's in use. For most product and service categories, needs are always being met. A lot of marketers make the mistake of thinking that everyone is always looking for a better widget. They're not. Better widget companies go out of business all of the time because it takes a lot to change habits and/or to undo process for the chance at more efficiency. Sure it's important to a prospect, but it's not always actionable.

REDUNDACY You've got to be a complete dolt not to run your old system while your new system is getting up to speed. The fact that it's important, and you have a good way to compare and contrast the redundancy, is comforting. Talk about that benefit. Comfort, security, trust … all important.

SCALABILITY FOR BUDGET No one has unlimited funds. The fact that you can scale your system to a budget is another huge plus. Shows flexibility and supports the fact that you won't make this person look stupid at some point for going down an unaffordable rabbit hole. Talk it up.

SCALABILITY FOR VOLUME Even though your system can do this well, the procurement person is likely not thinking about tomorrow, meaning getting significantly bigger as an organization. The CEO? That's a different story.

ON-SITE CODERS You don't supply it. Just be ready to counter. No need to address it in any formal communications. They don't really care anyway. It was probably the head of digital who put this up on the wall in the first place. Ha! Hidden agenda exposed.

MILESTONE GUARANTEES Hey, looks like you're not very good at meeting deadlines. Everyone knows that people tend to overestimate their own proficiency and self-worth, but the organization has some improving to do. Don't make it a messaging point.

INFORMATION SECURITY Ditto on shoring up internally. It's important to the prospect, but here the prospect might consider security to be table stakes. If you do well at table stakes, you should never make it a talking point unless you really, really, really hang your hat on it. For instance, a lot of organizations think they should feature "customer service." Don't, unless you're Nordstrom, or some other company that takes a commodity to extreme. Every company has customer service. Every one. People who leave an organization because of bad customer service will automatically assume any other company will deliver service better, and won't make their decision on a promise of extraordinary customer service. So unless information got egregiously breached, they're not going to give much of a shit for great information security. It's table stakes. Ignore it for primary messaging.

DATA SCRUB What's that? Well, let's just say that there are inconsistencies within an organization in regard to how part numbers are entered on purchase orders. If the E.R. orders TD06-75 (Tongue Depressor, six inch, three-quarter-inch wide), and the outpatient clinic orders TD0675, the two orders won't ladder up to a single contract because someone entered the part numbers differently. That's the data scrub. It's **HUGE**. Procurement people may not get the importance because they're not automating now. This is an opportunity to teach.

METRICS DASHBOARD Ditto on the opportunity to teach how important it is. Even though the gross generalization rule is "screw it, not important," in this instance it is. The procurement person may not know what they don't know.

INVENTORY MANAGEMENT This may not be what you're being hired for, but it might matter to someone … say, maybe, the CEO. Keep it in your back pocket as added value.

Those **NEEDS** were potential advertising messages or search messages on your website.

RFP CUSTOMER SERVICE There are lots of contact points in the RFP process to prove that you run a tight ship. When you're working with someone in the RFP stage, remember that they're looking for ways to **ELIMINATE** you not reasons to **CHOOSE** you. Don't fuck up. Don't be sloppy. Not much that you do to make them like you, or general schmoozing, will matter. Not fucking up the small stuff matters.

EASY TO UNDERSTAND RFP RESPONSE Looks, by this score, that you'll need to get better at being simple. Simple always wins. Always. Make whatever you give them look simple with good design (give it to an art person for fuck's sake), sound simple with short sentences (hire a writer to rewrite what your tech people wrote), and **DEMONSTRATE** simple with a pricing structure that's easy to understand (which tells them you've done this before and establishes trust). If you suck at this, get better immediately. Don't be delusional and think anyone will figure out that your product is better if your RFP response is sloppy and convoluted.

MAKE THEM LOOK SMART If you come off too smart when you're dealing with your prospect, which a lot of people actually try to do because they think it's impressive, stop. If you're a single point of contact, be accommodating. If you have multiple points of contact, designate your cast of characters to each have a role: one can be the nerd, but others have to have roles relating to buddy, buck-stops-here-leader, crazy innovator, fun person … your team should be a diamond, each occupying a facet, so sparkle can happen. And so your procurement person can latch on to someone who's not intimidating. Watch for whom they like and make sure that person has an important role. In regard to how you word your response, remember that you don't want them to feel stupid but supported. (Remember, all of the other marketing books are **CRAP**, and you, gentle reader, are super smart for buying and reading this one.

MAKE IT EASY It's already a hassle to change systems. **FOCUS** on easy, especially if you can deliver easy. Testimonials help here. **ON TIME**. Hardly anyone delivers on time. Heck, in some Asian countries they don't even have words for "on time," "deadline," "time sheet" and the like. When you think about it, what's time anyway? For a process like this, it's a weird admission of inferior quality. "We'll deliver on time" means "We'll put pencils down before it's done, so some functionality will be broken." Liberate yourself and others. Fuck time.

GOOD SUPPLIER FIND Well, lookie here, you have a brand problem! It's important to our procurement prospect's personal career to be associated with a winner, and either your reputation sucks, you don't come across with appropriate swagger, or you're a non-existent pile of meh. Get your brand act together, not for reasons of ego but for business survival.

Those **MOTIVATIONS** were why the company did or didn't choose you to advance your company to the finals of their process, or to choose you to get the contract.

NOW YOU NEED YOUR WISDOM TEETH PULLED

Yes, there's more (*"Stop! Stop! The team can't take anymore consensus!").* Now you need to do the CEO evaluation. But not to worry: The second time you do this version of numbers fun it goes a lot quicker. So much so that if you do more than two prospects, the thoughtfulness of the third prospect is really fast. So fast that it's usually garbage. It's not likely any campaign you do will have more than two prospects anyway, so don't even try. It's grueling, and most people just don't have the stamina (this includes the facilitator).

The CEO is an important juxtaposition, even if it's just because it's an iconic demonstration of the importance of empathy in marketing. Because you're now struggling to stay awake (thanks for plowing through), let's cut to the chase:

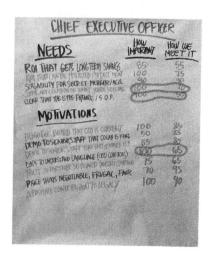

Circle insightful dispericies or curious thoughts.

NEEDS	HOW IMPORTANT	HOW WE MEET IT
ROI that translates to long-term cost savings	85	55
ROI that's easily projected and demonstrated for budget management	100	75
Scalability to accommodate secret merger/ acquisition	90	90
Clear articulation of what you're selling (because they might not be aware)	100	70
Clear reinforcement that this software is standard operating procedure of the hospital of the future	100	50

MOTIVATIONS	HOW IMPORTANT	HOW WE MEET IT
Demonstration to his/her Board of Directors that the CEO is ops-/tech- current	100	85
Demonstration to senior staff that there's an exception of collaboration	50	85
Demonstration to senior staff that performance standards are high	85	80
Easy-to-understand language, so the CEO dosen't feel out of control	100	65
Trust in a partner so his/her decision isn't questioned by the Board/staff	75	65
A price that demonstrates frugalness, ability to negotiate or fairness,	70	90
A positive contribution to their legacy	100	90

LONG-TERM ROI This is fucking fiction, and everyone knows it. It's important to the CEO because everyone asks for ROI like a knee jerk. There are so many variables that go into generating ROI equations that it's nearly impossible to be accurate on all of them, so, in effect, it's all bullshit long-term. And hardly anyone who's in the game today will be around long-term, so who cares? Where's the consequence? Plus, can we really predict variables that will come into play five years from now? And will all of these "savings" go into some piggy bank that gets broken and tangibly lands in someone's pocket one day? No. Please, everyone get real. Most small to mid-size companies don't have the math geeks to calculate ROI formulas, and it's not an agency's job.

PROJECTED BUDGET-BASED ROI This is more short-term. It's still bullshit fiction in that it's a projection, and the future cannot be accurately projected from the past without constant measurement and revision. ROI is a past-based process that's based on replication. For all of you nerds who do stats and are screaming right now, yes, there are formulas for decent prediction. That's why you get a nod here, given the shorter time frame. But one thing that should always be noted for new product innovations: It's new. The software is maybe new, as in not really tried-and-true in the sector to even qualify as "best practice." No past to replicate. Mind blown, heh?

SCALABILITY The procurement department won't always know about future mergers or acquisitions. Just assume every company these days will merge or be acquired. In the end, Amazon will own everything. You heard it here first.

CLEAR ARTICULATION CEOs aren't always aware of what's in the weeds. Not their nature. They like the future, so any messaging you do to CEOs has to connect the future to action they take today.

HOSPITAL OF THE FUTURE Ditto. The 50 score is because most companies when they communicate are very focused on their own value props. Especially B2B companies. The definition of "value prop" varies significantly, but this is a goodie: "What the prospect values." Now, if we take that definition as the value prop, you could argue that the CEO would value something bigger than "efficient operational transactions." Most companies' value props don't account for their role in prospect aspiration. They look down, and talk too much about the plumbing of their little widgets instead of the impact of their big kicks. (Did I spell something wrong?)

DEMONSTRATION TO THE BOARD CEOs get fired by their Boards. I've seen strong CEOs run around like crying toddlers in fear of their next Board meeting. Give CEOs talking points that help them position themselves as visionary by way of your product.

DEMONSTRATION TO SENIOR STAFF/COLLABORATION In a hospital, because that's what our prospect runs, most CEOs don't deal with day-to-day. So if, in your messaging, you talk a lot about how it'll bring departmental operations together, you're talking to the wrong person. That's the COO.

DEMONSTRATION TO SENIOR STAFF/STANDARDS Organizational excellence, however, is a big topic for CEOs. Like entrepreneurs, they achieve by surrounding themselves with great people, and when people lose their value they cut them out of their life. If you want lifelong loyalty, go work on a farm. In the business world, you're only as good as your last fail.

EASY-TO-UNDERSTAND LANGUAGE The CEO is smart, and they don't like to look dumb. We covered this earlier in the discourse; when you're selling, make everyone around you feel interesting, important, and captivating, and you'll make millions of dollars. That's eliminating your ego and stroking theirs.

TRUST Trust is more important at the other contact points because CEOs will defer to senior specialists. Some of this, which is why the 65, is related to brand. Per this exercise, we've established that the brand here needs some propping.

PRICE In every survey ever done for every product in the world, price is always something that's a perceived barrier. It's not. In fact, behavioral economics (which is the newish subset of psychology that integrates economic theory with consumer action) will tell you that the cheapest price is a disadvantage in choice architecture. Commonly, if you're buying something, you opt for "not too cheap but not too expensive" as a demonstration of thoughtful frugality. Don't race to the bottom.

LEGACY Most CEOs in hospital systems started with altruism. Helping people. That's all good, but inherent in that, people who sincerely help people often come to the conclusion that there's always more they could have done. Now combine that with the clawing, ruthless one-upmanship that often is necessary to rise in a large organization, and you have a cognitive dissonance that, as one ages, starts to feel like "What have I done? What have I accomplished?" Just a guess, and an observation, but hospital system CEOs are an interesting breed. They're accountable to and monitored for performance constantly by super smart people (physicians), they're exposed to life and death (patients), and they're responsible to their communities (latest, greatest equipment, plus ever-expanding services). Heavy. They deserve to feel like they've left a legacy. If the software platform does its job, it'll make a huge difference in efficiency and cost savings. As you communicate, play to it all.

ONE LAST MODULE. A FUN-ISH ONE.

It's the end of the day. Your group hates you. And the last impression of the day is how they'll view this experience. So if you've not yet brought out the chocolate or the margaritas, now's the time.

This last ditty is a fantastic exercise that requires a bit of pre-preparation, but it's positive, inclusive, and will allow you to tread water a bit because you, too, are exhausted. It's also an important component of the Creative Brief, and allows your group to cool down and synthesize what they've processed.

Give them a bathroom break, and while they're gone you're going to put about 75-100 (not exaggerating) words, hereby known, for sake of argument, as "adjectives" on a wall. When they return, you'll ask your group to narrow the wall down to **FIVE** words that define the tone of the creative expressions for the creative team. They'll need to come to consensus.

Prior to the day, you'll have purchased a pack of Post-it® notes, 8 inches by 6 inches. On each note, one word/thought exists, such as: **INNOVATIVE. SECURE. SAFE**. Go crazy, within reason and appropriate to the brand. **FIERCE. CONFIDENT. PROVOCATIVE.** Write big. **APPROACHABLE. IMAGINATIVE. TECHNICAL.** And have fun. **ELITIST. SOPHISTICATED. DARING.**

First, ask them to eliminate words. Take them off of the wall as they shout them out. If they don't like your words, they can add words. You write them, one at a time, on blank Post-it® notes and put them back up on the wall. Allow them to fight for words they love and discuss the merits of one word that may be more perfect than another.

This is their process but feel free to help them resolve issues in the end. Seven seems to be the roadblock. There are many psychological profiling systems and business/brand analyzers that use these kinds of attributes as a means for measurement. There are also methods to define brand archetypes, which are helpful in defining voice. This, albeit unscientific, is easy, simple, and good enough for campaign marketing purposes.

On the next page are some thought-starter words that I've used through the years. Many have made it to the five finalists. Have fun and have at it:

Reliable	Wholesome	Trendy	Current
Relentless	Seasoned	Gregarious	Humble
Hard-working	Youthful	Loyal	Thoughtful
Honest	Next-level	Trusting	Loving
Enthusiastic	Miraculous	Tenacious	Respectful
Smart	Brave	Competitive	Spontaneous
Fierce	Transformative	Real	Normal
Intelligent	Fast	Experienced	Fearless
Forward thinking	Furious	Inspiring	Scientific
Trustworthy	Intense	Insightful	Friendly
Provocative	Energetic	Objective	Controlled
Cheap	Patient	Accountable	Cheeky
Valued	Open	Brazen	Sarcastic
Approachable	Altruistic	Artistic	Senior
Technical	Righteous	Vivacious	Perfectionist
Organic	Serious	Passionate	Determined
Collaborative	Simple	Persistent	Ambitious
Buttoned-up	Complicated	Resolute	Practical
Innovative	Spirited	Proactive	Patient
Elitist	Ethical	High-status	Pure
Strong	Innocent	Authoritarian	Charming
Reputable	Deep	Tough	Motherly
Independent	Rugged	Nonlinear	Fatherly
Faithful	Successful	Aesthetic	Original
Nimble	Masculine	Eccentric	Curious
Nurturing	Feminine	Mannered	Indulgent
Whole	Tolerant	Meaningful	Superior
Comprehensive	Evolving	Dogmatic	Attractive
Positive	Joyous	Talented	Spiritual
Contrarian	Corporate	Adaptable	Beautiful
Flexible	Casual	Noble	Handsome
Risk-taking	Vivid	Traditional	Introspective
Hungry	Instinctual	Enlightened	Connected
Daring	Clever	Bubbly	Intuitive
Focused	Masterful	Non-toxic	Mysterious
Tireless	Useful	Optimistic	Pessimistic
Ingenious	Supportive	Orderly	Outlandish
Authentic	Resourceful	Stable	Moral
Leader	Type-A	Visionary	Balanced
Powerful	Tough	Natural	Courageous
Dependable	Sincere	Credible	Logical

Now, what does this massive pile of insight mean? You read about a detailed process, and if you took your time with this book you may have spent a couple of hours. If you lived it, between the SWOTT gathering and the team session, it was a few weeks with a couple of intense, mind-bending days.

So here's how you, as the marketer in charge, have changed: You know your product, the playing field, and the players like no one else. No one in your organization can challenge your 360-degree understanding of your brand's assets, liabilities, prospect expectations, and triggers. It's in your DNA. It's automatic muscle. Subconsciously, you, and you alone, see the path the brand has to traverse to move forward. Your helpers? They've only seen pieces of the vision that you've directed. They're ready to follow.

Time to swing the hammer, Thor.

DISCOURSE FIVE
HOW TO DIG FOR GOLD NUGGETS IN A PILE OF GOOD SHIT, OR WHY BRIEFS NEED NOT BE BRIEF

Simplify, simplify, simplify. Everyone in advertising hears it all of the time. Creative Svengalis stand on chairs and say, "What's the one thing? Give me the one thing and I shall give you brilliance!" Well, if it were one thing we could hire a monkey to be creative, but it would be demeaning to the monkey.

You've just read about a process that created a lot of information. A heaping pile of important-to-someone information that has now, if you're actually doing this process in real life, landed in your lap. How do you make sense of it? How do you make sense enough to stay true to the business, pay homage to the prospect, motivate and connect to your internal colleagues, and give the people who are creating marketing and advertising plans clarity of purpose?

Creating a brief, which is what you need to do, is essentially a report in various sizes, both vertical and horizontal. This process, in this book, is the basis for creating:

1. **A BUSINESS PLAN,** which is its full-on strategic motherlode of a birthing

2. **A MARKETING PLAN,** which is how, in part, the business plan is enabled (so, like, the business plan is the egg and the marketing plan is sperm ... nice metaphor, eh?)

3. **A BRIEF,** which is meant for the communications teams so they can do their respective jobs or MULTIPLE BRIEFS (read on)

4. **A DECK,** which has now become the generic term for just about any piece of internal communication because people can't write full sentences with proper grammar anymore, but that's okay because no one can read anyhow

The process of thinking here is like panning for gold. The information you've gathered is like water, both still and rushing, with little pieces of insight. The answers are on all that paper you just used: the Vision, the SWOTT, and Needs and Motivations. Take the papers, all of the papers, find a room (Your office? What? You're in one of those proven disfunctional open-concept offices? Reserve a private conference room for a week …), put the papers on the wall, and sit in the middle. Sit, for a long time, and take it in. Smell the sweetness of thought. Let the words surround you with reverence, meaning, and purpose. This is your cone of truth, Zen, and clarity.

During the meetings, you likely heard things over and over. The same Strengths, over and over. The same Weaknesses, over and over. The same Motivations, over and over. What were they? Trust? Innovation? Relationship? Those are three distinctly different things. **WHAT DID YOU HEAR OVER AND OVER?** What did everyone say, again and again until it became annoying? Hold that thought.

BRAND VS. PRODUCT

If you watch one of the multiple investor pitch shows, especially the one with investors named after fish, they sometimes choose not to invest by saying, "You have a product not a business." Is there a difference? Yes, there is, and the distinction between the two is important. Your brand is your business, and it's the voice that you'll speak in to send messaging by way of the benefits associated with the product or service you're selling. This is a big deal because it's where newbies to this thing get screwed up, and when people start to mutter, "We don't stand for anything." You may have internal operations, but you don't have a brand.

Figuring out how to create the cultural entity that is a brand, and its respective voice, is a book unto itself (which makes you excited about buying what's to come, right?). There are a lot of modules that people use to gain consensus about voice that, in turn, inform the brief that, in turn, informs an agency on tone. Tone and voice bring subjectivity into the creative process, and a lot of people who work client-side within an organization have a real problem with subjectivity, including CEOs. Which is one of the reasons data is revered, often at the expense of swagger; data is everywhere, but swagger is the mythic beast that a few people have, and the vast majority of humans couldn't find if their very existence depended on it. Like rhythm. Like knowing how to dance so you look good doing it.

THE BRIEF(S)

Swagger is what great brands are built on: soft and cuddly is swagger, confident and sexy is swagger, trustworthy and vigilant is swagger. Swagger isn't saying "trust us," because if you say "trust us" the last thing anyone is going to do is trust you. If you have to say it, you're not trustworthy. And you have no swagger.

"Hey, I'm just a peon at work. I bought this book because I hate my job. There's no way I'm going to assemble a team and run a fucking process." Fair. This fucking process works best with a team. But if you have no team **DO IT YOURSELF.** Do every bit of it **BY YOURSELF.** In fact, take this iterative 360-degree process and start applying it to your own life. New job, wedding planning ... get used to thinking this way, like a shortstop shags grounders over and over again. Automatic memory. People will start to say (not exaggerating), "How did you figure that all out so fast?" It's how to think in its fastest, most clarifying form. If you do this, you'll master your world and you'll no longer be a peon.

The most important thing you can do with this information is write a brief. Everyone in advertising has an opinion on the brief, which is why there isn't any right or wrong recommendation here. Since the beginning of advertising time, there are as many briefs as stars in the sky. Is one brighter than the other? Construct a brief format that's right for you and your team. We're going to assume, in this exercise, that you're briefing either your internal team or your agency to do communications for your software product for hospitals.

The brief is important because:

- It's the roadmap for where you're going as a product, and how that fits into where you're going as a company

- People will be spending hundreds, nay, thousands of hours working on what you tell them to do

- The brief will be how their thousands of hours will be judged

- If the brief is shit, everything they do will be shit, and it'll sort of be your fault

First, acknowledge that there are three different kinds of briefs.

1. There's the **BUSINESS BRIEF**, which makes a case for the product and its marketing. WHY you would even consider spending money on your widget, meaning its relevance to the market and to your company, happens here

2. There's a **CREATIVE BRIEF**, which is the map for creative thought, target profile, nod to the brand voice and position in the sector, purpose of the campaign in the higher order of business

3. Then there's the **PROJECT BRIEF**, which outlines things like budget, timing, communications components, who does what to get your campaign off the ground

A lot of people mix the second two together and forget about the first one, mostly because they're not always privy to the information. If possible, don't do that, because all briefs are important and you diminish their effectiveness by not giving each their deserved credit. You're also putting blinders on the people doing the work. Most people think a brief is just number three, which is easy nuts and bolts. But if you don't do number one, your boss bites you in the ass by asking at some point when everyone's spent a lot of time, "Why are we doing this again?" If you don't do 2, then creative people, forced to reckon with a blank sheet of idea paper, come up with stupid stuff, not because they're dumb but because they're making something out of nothing, and blind squirrels don't always find nuts.

So make an attempt to do all three briefs, even though some might find it overkill and aren't interested in reading all three. Doing all three, having them in your back pocket, gets your head together. Part of leadership, and feeling good about yourself, is putting in the work to know that you're right.

THE BUSINESS BRIEF

This is a format that's a great one-sheet base to answer the question "Why does any of this matter?" Yes, it's existential in that way, but it's the outside layer of that big onion you're peeling. If you've done the process, answering these questions is a piece of delicious cheesecake: a little thick and chewy, but satisfying. If you go to the website SmartCrap.com, you can download this little ditty electronically in a form. I've actually had people fill this out as part of a group process; that's hard, because most people, after the couple of exercises you just did with them have had enough of your reindeer games, and just want to go back and hide under their day-to-day blankets. Seriously, when your head's in the game, in your Zen war room, it goes down easy by yourself or with a couple of the people in your group who did good jobs (that is to say not everyone, but a select force).

BASE BUSINESS PLAN BRIEF

WHAT'S THE PRODUCT/SERVICE YOU'RE COMMUNICATING? You're like, "Seriously, this is the first question?" Yes, it is. The first question is asking you about what you're selling so you clarify to yourself, and others, that it's a product or service rather than a project that's trying to sell a relationship with an entire business or vice versa.

WHO ARE YOU COMMUNICATING TO? WHO IS YOUR PROSPECT? Remember that exercise where you outlined of all of the possible targets? Pick **ONE**. Fill this sheet out for that **ONE** target. Then, if you like, do another sheet if you plan on outreach to the other target and answer the same questions for that person.

WHAT'S THE SECTOR OPPORTUNITY? What? Left field? We haven't talked about the term "sector opportunity," sometimes called "market opportunity," before, but now that you're all info-lubed-up you'll be able feel the answer to this one in your intuition. Some condition has to exist in the market for your product/service to have a shot at succeeding. AKA an "unmet need." The sector opportunity is the reason why people might want to buy what you're selling that has nothing to do with your brand equities but, rather, everything to do with their situation. Now, there are me-too products everywhere; walk down a cereal aisle at the grocery store: There are a dozen chocolatey flakes, ricey things, globes, and weird squares, plus added chocolate bites to wheat/rice/corn-based carbohydrates. Is there really an unmet need for chocolate? Well, yes, because flavor profiles for chocolate vary significantly, and a cereal mavin may prefer one profile and/or shape/origin of carb to another. So unmet need? Yes.

Here's a big gross generalization that's also true: *Most new products and services fail because most needs are being met. "We've got a better widget" is what entrepreneurs say just before they lose millions of dollars.* If needs are met, it's crazy hard to get the masses to try something new, and then switch, and then keep up the switch, even if the product is better. Service is easier, in that the masses **LOVE** convenience and ease. They embrace those two because (remember "What's in it for me?") service benefits make people feel interesting, important, and in-the-know. Consumers will say it's time-savings, but, in reality, service benefits stroke an individual's ego. Better widget products don't. They're too logical, not emotional.

If you talk about unmet needs in the group, inevitably there's one smartypants who will bring up how Steve Jobs created and sold products to people who didn't know they had an unmet need. True, on the service. But read the previous paragraph. I'd argue that Apple did not create products but created **SERVICES** that stroked the ego of the buyers as elitist purveyors of the latest technology. They were first with that, and then everything after them became a product that tried to position to be a better widget. The products failed as services, and in the end people found out Steve made a pretty good needs-meeting widget after all.

KEY SUCCESS FACTOR This is what has to continue to happen in the market for your product to be successful. Most answers to this question are usually "everything needs to stay the same," as in no competitive threats rear their beautiful heads. The point of this question is to think defensively and acknowledge that you may not be the only team in the sector screwing around with papers on walls. As you advance, others advance. As you shore up, others shore up.

STRATEGIC OBJECTIVE/GOAL Some lexicon for you, so that you don't embarrass yourself when you start talking in front of someone who knows their shit:

AN OBJECTIVE is a state of being.
A GOAL is a number.

So when you say, "We want to be a leader in the sector" that's not a goal, that's an objective. When you say, "We want to gain five percent market share from our largest competitor by end of year," that's a goal, because it's numeric.

Put your objective or goal here, and think about the word "strategic" when you do it. Strategic means that your objective/goal is in context with something else, so "We want to be the best we can be" is an objective, but it's not strategic.

COMPETITIVE ADVANTAGE

Check the boxes here and elaborate.

__ **PRODUCT** Better widget?
__ **PRICE** Lower price?
__ **CONVENIENCE** Easer/faster for the prospect?
__ **SERVICE** Are you nicer than the other guys?
__ **MISSION** Is your competition evil and you're not?
__ **OTHER** Do you have some sort of added value?

If the answer is "none of the above," then just pack up your stuff and go home.

DECLARATION OF STRATEGY This is a sentence (if you're really good at clarity) or a paragraph (acceptable) that declares from all of the above the approach you're going to take to accomplish your business goal or objective.

Try this on for size and fill in the blanks:

> **"We are going to** _____(a play you're going to make)
> **in order to** _____(an effect you're going to have)
> **to get to this** _____(an objective or goal)."

Now you're probably wondering, "Shouldn't I have met with the team on that?" Yes, in real strategic planning, the team comes up with this. You can work with the team on a module that can come up with this, but it's hard to do it in a group. If you do, here's the formula:

1. Add another half day, a day or two after you finish with all the other stuff

2. Divide your team into groups if you have more than six people; three in each group

3. Give them the formula and let them figure it out with some prompts:

   - A play is an approach, a positioning, a pivot, an action

   - An effect is what happens after your play

   - What you're aiming for is to get something to happen to your company in the market

Have each mini-group present and come to consensus on what the strategy should be.

In the case of our B2B software product, here's a reasonable business strategy that might ladder up to a vision:

> *"We are going to focus our marketing and sales on small market hospital systems in order to capture 50 percent market share in hospitals under 300 beds to be acquired by and/or acquire our closest competitor in three years."*

This strategy gives everyone on the team some new clarity. Even though, for instance, your software can scale, it's a way bigger deal to win a huge hospital system. And the bigger the systems get, the more likely they'll do this kind of software processing themselves. So even though your competitor might be going after bigger systems, you're not, which brings clarity to whom you target and why. Having market share is a juicy morsel of equity when one entity is trying to eat the other to get bigger.

VISION FIT After you figure out your strategy, ask yourself, "Does it help make the Vision come true?" If the answer is NO, then it's a lousy strategy. Try again, and this time refer to the Vision.

RISK AND PITFALLS This is important, because nothing is a gimme. The answer should be in two forms: internal and external. This is an honest account of where you may step in shit as you proceed. They are factored by way of internal and external realities.

INTERNAL This is where the SWOTT rears its head, and the importance of good communication between the marketing department, operations, IT, and all other departments matters. For instance, your marketing strategy might be a good one, but if operations can't scale because HR sucks, you're screwed. In the case of this little hospital strategy, like getting four little fish rather than landing one big fish, you'll need multiple team leads who are all competent at onboarding a client. Does your SWOTT support that?

EXTERNAL This is where shoddy intel is identified. If you don't know what your competitors are up to, you lose. What has to happen that you can't control is simple defense, and as much as marketing is thought of as purely offense, understanding that you may need a "plan B" in your back pocket for covering your ass.

CRITICAL SUCCESS FACTORS The question here is, "What has to happen right in order for the strategy to be successful?" It's supposed to be the positive balance to Risk and Pitfalls, but it's easy to confuse the two. Critical success factors are a check to whether you have your Risk and Pitfalls correct.

INTERNAL Often this is a statement based on current states of being internally, such as current staffing. If your strategy's success, for instance, requires continued employment by a great onboarding manager, then it's good to note it. Your recommendation should include having his or her back rubbed by a professional masseuse once a week courtesy of the company.

EXTERNAL Many times this, too, is a statement of continuation. The flip side of Risk and Pitfalls, as in "We need no other, better, competitive platforms to miraculously enter the market, sponsored by Alphabet or some other Titan of Industry with more money and leverage than we have."

IDENTIFICATION OF SUCCESS Oh dear, here's where our friend "data" is factored. How will you know that your strategy and its corresponding execution did well? This is where, simply, you ask yourself if achieving the number is the definition of success, or if there are other shades of gray to success that make sense. "What success looks like" is something that evolves because success after six months is different than success after six years, and not everything needs to be a stated objective or a goal. It could be a byproduct, such as improved employee retention, the ability to attract new people to the organization, the ability to open another office on the other side of the country, etc. Think about your vision again and find ways to define soft but very real outcomes in addition to just revenue and profit.

THE CREATIVE BRIEF

This is an example of a great creative brief: Season Seven, Episode Six, "Game of Thrones," Jon Snow brings a crazed soldier of the dead, chained up in a box, to Queen Cersei Lannister and opens the box, and the sniveling zombie viciousness runs to try to eat Cersei, but the chain stops it from consuming her just in time. Then Jon makes the case that they should unite against the White Walkers. Boom! Creative brief.

Okay, so not a GoT fan? The point here is that there's a lot of obsessing in our world about creative briefs—structure and content— but briefs could be **ANYTHING**. Anything that motivates a "creative team" to understand why the assignment matters and gives them the tools to find messaging and channels to deliver a persuasive case to move a clearly defined prospect to action. It could be a video, a trip to the war room, a stunt, or, yes, a piece of paper. Point being, even though this chapter will offer a form designed to live on a piece of paper, don't limit your briefing if the spirit moves you.

The words "creative team" are in quotes because it's a common failing in the agency world to think that a creative brief is presented to a single creative director or group creative head, plus maybe a writer and an art director, and not **THE WHOLE** account team. That's arrogance and short-term agency containment at the expense of the right thing to do creatively. Remember that "need-to-know" rant earlier in the book, in that anyone (internally or externally) who's skimpy with defining who is, or isn't, worthy of information is actually power mongering?

With all due respect, any briefing about a campaign should include most of the entire account team:

- **ALL** creative people assigned: writers, art directors, designers

- **ALL** account people, to include the PMs (project managers)

- The media leads, like the lead strategy person and tactical buyer

- The social team, to include the lead and the actual person assigned to the account

- The digital lead and the person assigned to the account

- All researchers and planners assigned to the account

And who's running this little show? **YOU**, if you've managed this process (time to shine!). Overkill? **NO**, not if you're into "doing the right thing." If you're into doing the wrong thing, you'll have listened in the echo chamber of negativity that's human nature, rooted in laziness under the guise of cost savings. You'll have heard the voices … "too many meetings … waste of my time … I'm busy with other things … " Ignore them. This juncture—enlightening the people who actually do the work—is the most important part of the strategic process. Your deck, your business brief, however glorious, isn't what the prospect sees. What the team does is what will touch the prospect, and if they don't get it like you get it all of your work thus far is the real waste. It's a waste of time, consciousness, and potential.

When anyone starts a sentence with the words, "With all due respect … " what they really mean is that your relationship is such that they can't say, "Hey, asshole, you're wrong and here's why."

You don't own this party. You've created context, in that potential ideas are seeds. But all of this information now is worthless unless the seeds are planted in the minds of creators. Ideas can come from anywhere, and good ideas are advanced by specialty disciplines, also known as fertilizer (so getting called "a piece of shit" in this instance may not always be a bad thing). You're also now exposing people to an opportunity to learn, and in that they'll see you as a guru whether they admit it or not. So make attendance mandatory (no "I'll just read the deck" excuses) and warn them that they'll be there for about an hour, and it'll be time well spent. People will whine before the meeting, but I guarantee you no one will whine after the meeting. They'll feel important and flush with knowledge. And you? You're making it rain.

THE SCOURGE OF LITERACY: "THE ONE SHEETER"

There's a continuum. On one side, government documents written by conservative lawyers. On the other side, The One Sheeter, where every bullet point is a weapon of destruction pointed at nuance.

Yes, be brief. Yes, get to the point. But in that, you and the listeners in your briefing session, and the readers of your paper brief, need to acknowledge this one thing: Persuasion lies in the fringes not in the middle of a bullseye. If you're trying to MOVE a prospect to understanding/action, it's a MOVE, not a deepening of their current worldview, unless deepening their current worldview is what you're trying to do. In which case, then blast away at the obvious. Annihilate what's easy. But the secret to moving someone's perception is to understand everything about the context of what a prospect understands, what they're seeing besides your message, why what you do matters, how they need to change their thinking, what it means for them, and then how they take action. That's aiming off-center, and ideally it requires more than a one sheet brief.

The best creative campaigns I've ever been a part of had one thing in common: They all found a seed on the fringe and cultivated it. It may have come from someone in a focus group; or an off-handed client comment; or what was said over and over in a session that wasn't necessarily the main product attribute, but a frustration or a barrier that an organization hadn't yet overcome. At the risk of completely laying waste to incongruous metaphors, this is where creative gold is mined, and where trees with gold leaves sprout (insert the sound of nails on a chalkboard here).

In the last few decades, I've seen dozens of paper creative brief formats. There's no right or wrong, because briefs need to match the capacity of the team to understand. Which is why The One Sheeter is most people's preferred means of communication, in that it's the lowest common-denominator document.

So in the spirit of that, like the business brief, behold the creative brief in one glorious page:

THE BIG PICTURE This is a paragraph that condenses the business brief into a few salient sentences. What's the big business picture? Is the story about opportunity? Trend? Is it about a company on a roll or in trouble? How does this campaign support the organization's brand moving forward? Find your best Zen pillow and meditate on business context in your war room.

WHO'S THE PROSPECT AND WHERE ARE THEY AT?
This is the clearly defined prospect for our communications, by way of a demographic that the media department can use. If you don't know about demos, then ask a media person because these demos are very specific. Remember in our group process that we defined how this person thinks and what motivates them? Write a version of that here. In regard to "Where are they at?," this could be a current mental state, physical state, or challenge that they have that may help us solve a problem with our product.

WHAT DO THEY THINK ABOUT THE PRODUCT OR COMPANY? Do you have your intel yet? This is what the prospect believes to be true based on prior understanding, rumor, or history. It's possible they think nothing, which is an issue in awareness. In regard to awareness, **PLEASE, PLEASE, PLEASE** don't proclaim awareness to be the finished problem you're trying to solve or the objective of your campaign. That's so remedial. It's also highly presumptive on your part to think that if prospects were aware they would flock to purchase. They won't. Awareness has an evolved self, which is understanding. *"I am aware and I understand what your company stands for"* is a better prospect state to attempt to attain. To complete the trifecta, strive for your prospect to think, *"I am aware, I understand, and I know why your company matters to me."* Conversely, if your prospects are already aware be sure to outline here why they dismiss your product or company from consideration. This is the spot on the map that'll mark the beginning of your communications journey.

WHAT DO WE WANT TO CHANGE ABOUT WHAT THEY THINK ABOUT THE PRODUCT OR COMPANY? Which is the logical follow-up to the previous point about the map. Spatially it matters because you need to know what direction to go in your communications. If they think your company is an "untested start-up" that's a different messaging path, in a different direction, than simply "unaware." Or, if your product had performance issues in the past, it's good to know that you're overcoming objections rather than simply putting information out there for blind consumption.

WHAT ARE THE THREE PILLARS OF THE BRAND?

Here's where you need to know a bit about what you stand for as an organization. If there's one pillar, so be it, but if there's five, cut it to three. What promises, as an organization, do you make to your customers? Most companies have mission mantras or CEO runoff that'll sometimes hit a poster in the lunchroom. Sometimes tricky marketers refer to stuff like this as "brand DNA." Here are common thoughts to jump-start your answer: honesty, innovation, customer service, customer-centered decision-making, efficiency, made in the U.S.A., integrity, craftsmanship … you get the idea.

WHAT ARE THE THREE PILLARS OF THE PRODUCT?

If the brand is the business, then the product might have different pillars than the organization. For instance, a large holding company might have product lines that occupy high-, medium-, and low-end price points, so the pillars of the product may change significantly. These pillars may impact product positioning, such as "accessibly priced" if the big deal is that it costs less, or "easy to use" or "convenient." Brands aren't easy to use, products are. That's how you tell the difference.

WHAT'S THE COMPETITIVE CONTEXT? So many briefs that I've seen from other agencies, and brands, completely forget that there's a big world out there, and our product is going to be viewed in context. Depending upon how you choose to provide fodder for this answer, you could attach competitive advertising and/or a competitive review of product/messaging to your document as basis here. Also consider the questions: Whom are we compared to? By what measures do we win or lose in comparison? And at the end of the day, what box will we be put in? For our hospital platform, this is where "We're the safe choice vs. the innovative choice" comes into play.

WHAT ARE THE ADJECTIVES THAT DEFINE OUR PERSONALITY? Here's where the fun assignment at the end of your grueling day matters. Anything creative that the team does should be internally vetted by way of these words. It helps them, and if they go off track it's way better than saying to creative people, "Ah, I just don't like it" when they present something stupid. Refer to the brief, this brief, ask them if they believe the expression reflects the emotion found in these words. They'll appreciate your specificity and won't tag you as ineffectual because you can't articulate what you want. Never say, "I'll know it when I see it." OMG, you'll need to quit, change your name, and move to another city because you'll never live it down as a client in the creative community.

HOW DO WE KNOW WE'RE ON THE PATH TO SUCCESS? Here's where you outline your goals (with numbers) and your objectives (states of being). "We'll know we're on the path to success when we've generated five RFP requests, ideally within the first two months after our campaign launch." Does that all sound squishy? It's supposed to. It's remarkable that in an age where most professional people are familiar with the term "continuous improvement," most campaign goals set initiatives up for one-point-in-time binary success or failure. Life isn't black and white, it's 500 shades of gray, to include warm and cool gray, dove gray, battleship gray, and gunmetal gray. That's not to say that we should eschew the expectation of performance. Otherwise, why bother? But continuous improvement, by definition, means there's no end point to disciplined action. Bury the bar, yes, mostly so you can keep running over it quickly.

WHAT'S THE DO THING? I love this. As a brand strategist, this simple trick has rocked my world. Answer this question: If the product was a verb, what does it do for the prospect? Open the skies and let the rays of light shine down because a lot of what creative people need to do is found right here. When I don't have the benefit of a daylong planning session with a client and have to figure something out quickly, this is where I start. Secret revealed! If the product was a verb, what does it do for the prospect? Answer, in the case of our little B2B software platform: *It makes them feel effortlessly in control.* Not a bad basis for a campaign, no matter if you're talking to the CEO or Procurement.

WHAT'S THE ONE THING? PLUS MANDATORIES. After years in the business romancing the delicacy of insight and the playful patterns of human behavior on the canvas of the human psyche, in the end a lot of people, after just an hour of strenuous, mind-numbing calisthenics, look up from the floor, beaten, thirsty, exhausted and say, "I give up. What's the one thing?" Sure, what the fuck. Give them the One Thing, if you have it. Look to the Do Thing, and maybe add a couple of product-based bullet points. But know that they heard you on the rest of it, and their work will be more compelling and effective because of it.

> Who fills out the creative brief? Great question. Most often, when a client has an agency, it's the agency strategist, planner, or senior account service person who creates the brief. Then, before the brief is presented, the client blesses it. If you're in a progressive agency, creative directors may also weigh in on the brief before it goes to the client, as a gut check that creative can actually be developed off of the brief (meaning, are there enough emotional cues embedded and is there clear creative intent?). Clients with in-house departments obviously do their own briefs. The question really is, who ran the process? That's the all-knowing person who should write the brief.

THE PROJECT BRIEF

Here's the brief that answers the question the creative people ask most often, which is, "What am I doing again?" It's a little bit like the chicken and the egg, in that you've just invited your media and social people to the briefing, and ideally they might have ideas that significantly change the scope of work. It's all a give-and-take when it's done well. You may want to consider creating this piece especially, in Google Docs to accommodate updates in real time.

CLIENT/PRODUCT CAMPAIGN NAME TEAM

___ MARKETING/ACCOUNT SERVICE/
PROJECT MANAGEMENT

___ CREATIVE

___ SOCIAL/CONTENT

___ MEDIA

___ OTHER SPECIALTIES: RESEARCH, DIGITAL,
PR, PROMO, ETC.

ASSIGNMENT

TARGET

PRELIMINARY MEDIA TO BE USED

NUMBER OF EXPRESSIONS

TIMETABLE

___ PLANNING DELIVERABLE REVIEW

___ PRESENTATION OF BRIEFS TO TEAM

___ QUESTIONS/REGROUP/CHECK-IN

___ FIRST CONCEPTUAL REVIEW/INTERNAL
(CREATIVE + CONTENT/SOCIAL)

___ SECOND CONCEPTUAL REVIEW/INTERNAL
(CREATIVE + CONTENT/SOCIAL)

___ MEDIA REVIEW/INTERNAL

___ CONCEPT PRESENTATION/EXTERNAL
(ALL DISCIPLINES)

___ MEDIA DEADLINES

PAID MEDIA SPECIFICATIONS

___ PRELIMINARY SPECIFICATIONS

___ FINAL SPECIFICATIONS

EARNED MEDIA DIRECTIVES

OWNED MEDIA DIRECTIVES

BUDGET/HOURS RECAP

___ BUDGET PER SPECIALTY

MANDATORIES (CALL TO ACTION, URL, CONTACT INFORMATION, ETC.)

SO, THEN, WHAT'S THE BRIEFING MEETING LIKE?

So everyone has replied that they'll be attending your one-hour party. There will be people from all disciplines, each with a small chip on their respective shoulders because you're making them attend a long (maybe even an hour-and-a-half) meeting.

Most people like having a horizontal presentation vehicle, commonly referred to as a deck. For what it's worth, when you format something horizontally it does have a certain gravitas that vertically formatted words do not.

A few tips about your presentation:

1. If the deck is being presented on a monitor or screen, keep it simple. Super simple. Like, minimum of 36 point type simple with lots of white space. Limit your words to prompts and speak to the prompts. At this point, you've done so much work on this that you know it all by heart, so don't be nervous. You've got this

2. Begin your presentation by outlining/thanking everyone who participated in the process, from the SWOTT to the "research" interviewees to the participants. This is basically a throw-down that this isn't your thoughts but the thoughts of many stakeholders. Not-to-be-challenged stakeholders

3. Explain the process something like this: "We used a 360 process where we looked at the marketing challenge from nearly every perspective. We went beyond simple product attributes, considering all target audiences and key influencers, competitors, the needs and motivations of the highest-priority targets, the brand in its competitive space, and how the initiative you're about to learn about today is critical to the organization's future." Yikes! Holy crap! Yes, that's what you just did

4. Explain that they'll walk out with three briefs, if that's what you've decided to share: A Business Brief that'll give them context for how important this is to their organization. A Project Brief that'll be continually updated with specifics about the campaign and deadlines

and a Creative Brief that'll help the entire team begin the process of ideation

And then, for the next hour, present your briefs in that same sequence: Business, Project, Creative. The reason you want to end with Creative is that you want them to view the creative in the context of the media vehicles outlined in the Project Brief. By that time they'll be percolating already. Hand the briefs out as paper, so they can read them privately and not on a screen. Add spot color to important phrases, such as The One Thing or The Do Thing. If you feel you really nutted the Creative Brief, consider laminating it—seriously—because laminating makes everything better.

SO HOW HAS THIS REDUCED THE SHITSHOW OF MY WORK LIFE?

This is a recipe for the strategic execution of a marketing initiative from start to finish. It's also a recipe for an operations audit, the presentation of an idea you might have that'll get lost or misunderstood by your boss if you just tell them, or a personal self-evaluation of your life when you make yourself the client. It's how to think from every perspective, to make a challenge dimensional and hold it in your hands for observation. Look above it, look below it, look at it from the inside out and the outside in. What do you see?

When the shitshow is happening, what can you control and what can't you control? What role do you play in the game? Is it possible you'll play better if you can make internal communications clearer? Or is the issue you?

Have *you* now evolved?

SMARTCRAP.COM

BUSINESS BRIEF

WHAT'S THE PRODUCT/SERVICE YOU'RE COMMUNICATING? _____

WHOM ARE YOU COMMUNICATING TO? WHOM IS YOUR PROSPECT? _____

WHAT'S THE SECTOR OPPORTUNITY? _____

KEY SUCCESS FACTOR _____

STRATEGIC OBJECTIVE/GOAL _____

COMPETITIVE ADVANTAGE

__ **PRODUCT** Better widget?
__ **PRICE** Lower price?
__ **CONVENIENCE** Easier/faster for the prospect?
__ **SERVICE** Are you nicer than the other guys?
__ **MISSION** Is your competition evil and you're not?
__ **OTHER** Do you have some sort of added value?

DECLARATION OF STRATEGY

"WE ARE GOING TO _____ (A PLAY YOU'RE GOING TO MAKE)

IN ORDER TO _____ (AN EFFECT YOU'RE GOING TO HAVE)

TO GET TO THIS _____ (AN OBJECTIVE OR GOAL)"

VISION FIT _____

RISKS AND PITFALLS

INTERNAL   EXTERNAL

_____   _____

_____   _____

_____   _____

_____   _____

CRITICAL SUCCESS FACTORS

INTERNAL   EXTERNAL

_____   _____

_____   _____

_____   _____

_____   _____

IDENTIFICATION OF SUCCESS _____

CREATIVE BRIEF

THE BIG PICTURE _____
_____
_____

WHO'S THE PROSPECT AND WHERE ARE THEY AT? _____
_____
_____

WHAT DO THEY THINK ABOUT THE PRODUCT OR COMPANY? _____
_____

WHAT DO WE WANT TO CHANGE ABOUT WHAT THEY THINK ABOUT THE PRODUCT OR COMPANY? _____
_____
_____

WHAT ARE THE THREE PILLARS OF THE BRAND?   **WHAT ARE THE THREE PILLARS OF THE PRODUCT?**

1. _____   1. _____

2. _____   2. _____

3. _____   3. _____

WHAT'S THE COMPETITIVE CONTEXT? _____
_____
_____

WHAT ARE THE ADJECTIVES THAT DEFINE OUR PERSONALITY? _____
_____

HOW DO WE KNOW WE'RE ON THE PATH TO SUCCESS? _____
_____
_____

WHAT'S THE DO THING? _____
_____
_____

WHAT'S THE ONE THING? PLUS MANDATORIES. _____
_____
_____

PROJECT BRIEF

CLIENT/PRODUCT CAMPAIGN NAME _____

TEAM

___ MARKETING/ACCOUNTANT SERVICE/PROJECT MANAGEMENT
___ CREATIVE
___ SOCIAL/CONTENT
___ MEDIA
___ OTHER SPECALTIES: RESEARCH, DIGITAL, PR, PROMO, ETC.

ASSIGNMENT _____

TARGET _____

PRELIMINARY MEDIA TO BE USED _____

NUMBER OF EXPRESSIONS _____

TIMETABLE

PLANNING DELIVERABLE REVIEW _____

PRESENTATION OF BRIEFS TO TEAM _____

QUESTIONS/REGROUP/CHECK-IN _____

FIRST CONCEPTUAL REVIEW/INTERNAL (CREATIVE + CONTENT/SOCIAL) _____

SECOND CONCEPTUAL REVIEW/INTERNAL (CREATIVE + CONTENT/SOCIAL) _____

MEDIA REVIEW/INTERNAL _____

CONCEPT PRESENTATION/EXTERNAL (ALL DISCIPLINES) _____

MEDIA DEADLINES _____

PAID MEDIA SPECIFICATIONS

PRELIMINARY SPECIFICATIONS _____

FINAL SPECIFICATIONS _____

EARNED MEDIA SPECIFICATIONS _____

_____

OWNED MEDIA DIRECTIVES _____

_____

BUDGET/HOURS RECAP

BUDGET PER SPECIALTY _____

MANDATORIES (CALL TO ACTION, URL, CONTACT INFORMATION, ETC.) _____

_____

_____

You can download these, built in a Microsoft® Word file, at SmartCrap.com.
FREE! Because you already bought the book.

FINAL DISCOURSE

THE ZONE

ONE STEP INTO THE ZONE

Marketing is about you. The visionary. It's not data. It's not tactics. It's you and the quality of what you see.

What you see is what you consume. The Zone is a meditation; creativity is a breath you take in, let simmer, and expel into thought. It's a miracle of multiplicity: learnings, context, influence. It isn't information as much as it is connecting into the wisdom of ages. Like the iron in your blood, you're part of the cosmos, the Big Bang, the stars of galaxies past, except it's thought: learnings, context, influence.

What have you learned? What did you learn today? What has imprinted on you is part of what you exhale. There's an illusionist, a hero of mine, Derren Brown. Go to YouTube and search for his "Advertising Agency Task" video. He does an experiment with two advertising creative people. He puts them up in a hotel for the night, under the pretense of making a video. He sends a car to pick them up and bring them to his office. Then he asks them to concept (ad people's word for "make some conceptual ideas") a campaign for a client that he tells them about for the first time. They do their thing and then present to him. After the presentation, Darren takes out a sealed envelope that holds an eerie prediction of what the two creative folks just came up with. (Read on to eventually find out the trick.)

Your thoughts are what you see. What you consume becomes your consciousness. What have you consumed lately and throughout your life? What's your exposure?

You're now starting to think you're powerless, right? Well let's talk a bit about power. ... We've all heard the axiom "Information is power." In the context of the shitshow that is your professional life (getting back to why you bought this book), "Information is power" shows up every day in all of the assholes who tell you that you're not on the "need to know" status list. Or they know a digital trick you don't. Or they only tell you about your part of a task, rather than the reason why the task is important and needs completion. Or they keep their agency in the dark because the agency wouldn't directly use the information, or shouldn't know sales performance numbers or company vision. Are you one of these assholes? Or are you the target of this shit, in your own department, in your own way, in your organization?

People who hold information as power, as in your bosses or your clients, have little dick souls.

People who learn, share, learn, share, learn, share are people who live in the Zone. And in the Zone they know that whatever prize piece of knowledge or idea they have today will be replaced by a more magnificent idea tomorrow. So "knowledge is power" doesn't apply. Shared consciousness has way more power than any trick or nugget of info du jour.

It's your job, as the mind that stands before the fan that's blowing shit in every recess of your self-esteem, to rise above and control your own consciousness: learnings, context, influence.

What you learned in this book of how to do simple strategic planning with a group was sneaky step one in directing the consciousness of the group around you, for the purpose of giving you context in which to think, and giving others context in which your ideas will be viewed.

That's right, you manipulator, you. You just created a group exercise that enabled you to direct the thoughts of the people around you by manipulating the legitimacy of what you'll next present to them, which is a strategic direction founded in group collective consciousness (but mostly if you did it right, **YOUR** consciousness). You put your figure on the scale of weighty ideas. Will it work in the short-term? Who the fuck knows? It's better than having you or, God forbid, some operations or digital tactician person pull some shit out of their ass. But long-term, it worked because you just got a taste of letting go in order to ride the Zone like you're on a surf board. The wave is in control, but you're the one on top. You move the collective consciousness of your organization and your organization's brand. Like a boss.

Meetings are also old-school but inherently good for clarity. One of the disciplines most important to your Zone training as a marketing guru is respect for proper communication. There's this thing called Mehrabian's formula that (overfuckingsimplification, but that's okay because it's what you'll remember) says that 7 percent of a construct's meaning is in the words spoken, 38 percent of meaning is paralinguistic (how words are spoken), and 55 percent is in the facial expression of the person saying it.

For instance, the way you say "What the fuck!" matters a lot to its meaning, and, intrinsically, you communicate meaning not through the three words but how you say the phrase and what you look like when you say it.

Which brings us back to what you've consumed lately.

If you pay attention in school, you learn a lot, like that formula for meetings. Over time, it simmers down like a reduction sauce, thickening and intensifying its flavor, which becomes your wisdom, your intrinsic knowledge. In college, there was a sociology professor who said very little I could understand—thick, Panamanian accent that pronounced "focus" as "fuck us," which changed the meaning of his content considerably, but I got what he was trying to say because I sat in front and watched his hairy bearded Mehrabian mug—but he said some words that stuck with me forever: "*If you know one more thing than someone else, you are an expert.*" True dat. What a prediction. One more thing. So how are you getting that one more professional thing, oh, aspiring marketer? What will your one more thing be, and what have you consumed lately?

For instance, did you go to business school? Did you learn about **IF>THEN** in math? Here's one for you: **IF** you did, **THEN** you got a lot to learn about marketing communications to humans because it's all based in psychology: Erik Erikson's stages of psychosocial development. Maslow's heirarchy of needs. Nudge theory, AKA behavioral economics, which is finally starting to invade how people price products and promotions, for instance.

Other business bridges have developed. Have you explored the works of David Kolb? He's not a CEO, he's a learning theorist, and I'm going to reeeeeally bastardize and simplify his work here. So don't sue me David; I'm adding experiential learning (ha!) to your philosophy. (And if you're a fan of this shit, my next book will simplify/bastardize/liquify all sorts of wisdom for everyday marketing use. Holy crap I better start writing. Too many book promises ...)

So basically what Kolb said was that people learn four different ways: they feel it and experience it (sensitive, creative empaths), they watch it and think it (logicians, data junkies, abstractionists), they do it and think it (technical, practical types), and they feel it and do it (basically, everybody else who listens to their gut and doesn't work really hard thinking, which is **MOST PEOPLE**). Why does this matter?

It matters two ways:

YOUR STRATEGY MEETING, THE THING WE TALKED ABOUT IN THIS BOOK (FOR THOSE OF YOU WHO ARE SHORT-TERM-MEMORY DEFICIENT) If you did it right, you embedded nuggets for each of these learners. Even using color, playing music during breaks, going around the room to ask watchers what they think, putting people in groups to solve problems, handing someone process tasks in which they can participate, tossing in metaphors, making them review competitive messaging that's visual - all are catalysts for specific learning styles. Not everyone learns rationally, and there are lots of people who won't remember **ONE WORD** of the Excel handouts you give them for reference, preferring to latch on to group think or metaphorical think. You need to engage them for their input is valuable.

YOUR EVENTUAL MARKETING MIX Because people learn in ways that range from kinesthetic (those people who need to work with their hands, experiment, and collaborate) to visual pictures with music to words to diagrams, you've got to present communications in ways that most closely align with your audience set. If you're selling software to geeks, well, they might not watch an anthemic, beautiful, music-driven YouTube spot unless it's a Star Wars trailer. But if you're trying to influence most people—consumer marketing—you better have human pictures with a voiceover and auditory imprinting device in the mix, because they're not going to read your chart. Is this common sense? **YES**, based on academic research. But you'd be surprised how many marketers scoff at radio (feel it/do it) because it "doesn't work" or print (watch it/think it) because "no one reads anymore." Yes, people do listen to radio commercials and do read magazines. They subconsciously process the information that invaded their peripheral consciousness and, unknowingly, act on it.

Learnings, context, influence. You've just consumed something that may, with nurturing, change your life forever. Now you'll watch for different learners, test how you communicate with them, or, at the very least, use what you just learned as one more thing to position yourself as an expert in your next meeting of Shitshow Marketers Anonymous.

FLOW, AS IT RELATES TO THE ZONE

If you're reading this, you might be one of the millions of people who has watched Mihaly Csikszentmihalyi's TED talk on Flow, or maybe you've read an article or a book about it. But probably not either, since the whole Flow thing is more than a decade old and YouTube is now for cats. But you should seek it out, because the Zone, by any other construct, is Marketing Flow, combined with what happens when you just accumulate input, sometimes referred to as crystalized intelligence (or just, "the stuff you know but you don't know where it came from").

Flow was named Flow because those who experienced it described it as water, rushing, taking you to a place of merged action and awareness based on a presence of high performance. It's a high, a success high, that athletes feel when they're at the top of their game. Pitchers feel it when they throw strikes, point guards feel it when they drill threes, runners feel it when they fly fast without exhaustion. Flow is an intellectual thing too, in that what you expose yourself to—learnings, context influence—is fuel for Flow. It simmers in your head, it starts to make sense subconsciously, and it comes out when you need it most. Have you ever had moments when you get a lot of things done? When you see critical execution paths to a project in a fourth dimension, like you have an instantaneous map in your head for time and process in order to make a deadline? When you're able to give the people around you the exactly right direction in a split-second's time, pulled out of your ass, and you think, *"Damn, I'm good, and no one knows it except for me"*? That's Flow. That's part of how you get to the Zone.

THE OTHER PART OF THE ZONE: EMPATHY

You're in charge. You're the leader of your world, your personal planet of self-esteem and accomplishment. You're also the leader of an area of dominance at work. A cog, you say? No, you have a sphere of influence at work, and your ability to lead professionally is absolutely tied to your ability to access the energy of the Zone.

The oxymoron here is that as you lose yourself in the music, the moment, you own it ... (oops, just lost myself in song) ... as you lose yourself, you find yourself. It's through getting into the minds of others that, in turn, blows your mind up to see things others can't (like attack ships on fire off the shoulder of Orion? Oh you **NERD!** ...) because in marketing you can never forget that you're creating a reality that doesn't yet exist. The Vision from the first planning module? Professionally, that's your guidepost, your measure of success, and your map for taking the next step and the next 1,000 steps as a marketing professional in service to your organization and/or client.

What we're creating, beyond a measurable state of revenue or a measurable state of influence (in the case of non-profit advocacy, for instance) is a brand. There are lots of definitions of **BRAND**, and they can be verbs, nouns, or adjectives. This is the definition that has served me well. As you think about your Vision and the construct of empathy, consider this:

A BRAND IS AN EMOTIONAL RELATIONSHIP WITH THE MIND OF THE PROSPECT Huh? Yes. Empathy. What does someone think now, and how do my actions give their perception the appropriate heave-ho to get my product to where the Vision dictates it should be? That's all empathy and understanding the nuances to get the brand to be an appropriate expectation in the client's mind.

Note that this is NOT an intellectual relationship. It's an emotional one. Because even if you're one of those Kolb technical practical types, you still love, hate, and open or close your mental doors to persuasion. For the record, the intellectual relationship that's in the mind of the prospect is a position not a brand. (Remember that from the list of who gets invited to RFP parties? Those are positions not brands.)

To recap: Your job as a marketer is to get into every prospect's head and manipulate it. You're a marketer if you're a client, an account service person, a media buyer, a social specialist, a writer, an art director, or an intern. That's your job. That's your athletic role. And to do that, you'll live, work, and play in the Zone of left/right, up/down, unconscious consciousness of cultural, intellectual input that has inspired everyone from James Joyce to Beyoncé.

James Joyce: "I am tomorrow, or some future day, what I establish today. I am today what I established yesterday or some previous day."

Beyoncé: "I sneezed on the beat and the beat got sicker."

Okay, fine, truth be told an appropriate Beyoncé quote was hard to find, but she does flow, and no one can put their finger precisely on it but she does know how to work the Zone as one of the world's foremost marketers. Sneezing on the beat is the output of her combined consciousness.

SO WHAT DOES THAT ALL MEAN? THIS WHOLE BOOK?

"Hey, yikes, I bought this book to learn some skills because I hate my job, and now I'm expected to change the world?" you say. Answer: Yes. Let's recap with new words:

1. You're a powerful force. You're a marketer. You can create that which does not exist: culture, revenue, opinions, and conduct. Your actions can save lives, literally and metaphorically. You have the ability to do the single most important thing in the world: persuade others to do or think something. (Persuasion will be

the topic of the next book in the series ... promises, promises)

2. You likely work in a place that doesn't understand your potential and the secret that you now know. Still, hone some skills where you are. Start by adding value to the people who sign your check if you're an employee. If you're a CEO, learn to cultivate your talent and understand when to access input outside of your organization. No one wants to work for a frugal loser; strive to win. If you're an agency, understand that your responsibility, too, is to serve. Begin by asking the right questions, even if your client doesn't want to answer them. Whomever you are, your happiness, self-esteem, and proficiency as a marketer is on you and no one else

3. Share your brain, your reasons why, and what you've learned. Reveal your innermost secrets to others. Agencies, tell your clients how they can work with you better. For instance, if you're underpaid, find a way to let your clients understand how together you can move to equitable. Clients, set your internal and external departments up for success. Everyone: Don't be jerky people, and hold hostility or information inside. It's not conducive to connecting to the collective consciousness of the Zone, which is a positive force

4. Find a way to think like whom you're not, to see and learn from different POVs, but also to understand triggers so you can, at some point, persuade others who aren't like you. Understanding the motivations and worldview of your prospect audiences is key to moving them in a direction by your command. Find out how they learn. Then, be ready to persuade them to come to the conclusions that you want them to have. (Only use this knowledge for good and not evil)

5. Understand that some people just aren't cut out for strategy, and if you are you're special. Special in that you see a future that does not exist, and with training you can move people to aim in the direction of that future and run. If you're not strategic, you're still important. You're the runner, and no one gets anywhere without you

6. Think by way of 1. Sequence, 2. Collaboration, 3. Fodder for wisdom. For sequence, don't peel onions from the middle but, rather, from the outside in. Think about the entirety of the communications challenge, to include the reason why any/all of it may matter. Second, collaborate with others to understand their POV and to get them not to hate you. People don't like visionaries because they come off as holier-than-thou elitists who are smarter than the greatest minds of all time. Okay, fair. However, if you really do listen to others, and attempt to honestly understand their personal motivations, you're in the land of win-win when you suggest solutions, and that's the definition of greatness. Last, get smart. Start reading, listening to podcasts, seeing movies outside of your comfort zone, **ANYTHING** to broaden your base of knowledge in order to provide fuel for the Zone. You are what you mentally consume. Stay away from junk food, such as reality TV and the darkness that is today's news. It can make you crazy, in a bad way

OKAY, GOT IT. HOW DID THAT ILLUSIONIST KNOW THOSE AD GUYS' THOUGHTS?

He manipulated their thinking. He didn't know their thoughts. Seriously, go to YouTube and take a look. From the hotel to the location of the presentation in the car, the route was seeded with images, shapes, and words that imprinted the creative people. Did they know it? No. Because 85 percent of communication is subliminal, and you're taking it all in by way of your exposure, as innocently as what street you drive down and what visual, written, and auditory expressions greet you along the way. Influential context surrounds us. Even advertising people, who think that they're purposefully aware of imagery, are influenced, and they don't know it's happening to them. Protect yourself, protect your children, and fill your senses to reflect whom you want to be. Because it is that person whom you'll become.

Good luck, Godspeed, and buy the next book.

XO Denise

Denise's current agency is House United,
a strategy and creative consultancy that works on behalf
of both agencies and brands directly.

For more information and contact information,
check out thehouseu.com.

CPSIA information can be obtained
at www.ICGtesting.com
Printed in the USA
BVOW08s2242191217
503281BV00016B/1064/P